AM I THE ONE YOU ARE LOOKING FOR?

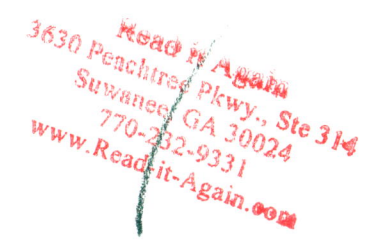

JAMES L. CRAWFORD

ISBN 978-1-0980-5871-5 (paperback)
ISBN 978-1-0980-5872-2 (digital)

Copyright © 2020 by James L. Crawford

All rights reserved. No part of this publication may be reproduced, distributed, or transmitted in any form or by any means, including photocopying, recording, or other electronic or mechanical methods without the prior written permission of the publisher. For permission requests, solicit the publisher via the address below.

Christian Faith Publishing, Inc.
832 Park Avenue
Meadville, PA 16335
www.christianfaithpublishing.com

Printed in the United States of America

Preface

My wife and I live in the Midwest in a small community in a rural area. We lead a simple life with our families as we all live nearby. We attend an Orthodox church with many friends and clergy.

I'm writing this book for the addicted person that has hope or no hope, no matter how small or great, that someday or some way, he or she may be able to break out of the darkness that surrounds our way of life. To enter in to the light, a new life, a joyful life, finding a new love.

Letting the real you, the inner you, the one inside that wants to be free and be in control of our life, not the one on the outside who puts on the same face every day.

This new life will bring forth a new love, a deep love, a kinder, simple, but very deep love. A love that understands the causes of suffering and sorrow, a love that firmly resists the passions of the world today.

Love that is wise varies according to your disciplining yourself and then reaping the rewards of a hard-fought battle; casting our cares upon the Lord, we can make every day a success. As time passes you will grow wiser, and with respect to the Lord's dealing with us, we will be instructed in many different ways to acquire wisdom.

The Lord's wisdom, the never-ending power of knowing, will be given to you and you can now subdue the passions that will try to destroy our life.

"Lord Jesus Christ, Son of God, have mercy on me, a sinner."

Amen.

Memorial to James L. Crawford

As a boy, James lived in a small town in the Midwest with his parents and three sisters. His parents divorced when he was twelve years old; he moved with his mother to a place in the country where he attended a one-room schoolhouse. During the summer, at the age of fourteen, he joined the community 4-H club to meet this *cute girl* he had been attracted to in the neighborhood. They ended up both attending the same high school together in the nearby village.

He served in the National Guard prior to joining the United States Army in 1954. He served in Germany with the 5th Infantry Division Heavy Weapons and 7th Army Rangers. He was discharged in 1956, rejoined the National Guard, and married that cute girl in their hometown. He was blessed with four children, two sons, and two daughters, living a happy normal life.

In 1972, he bought a store and began a small business. He worked very hard and long hours to have a successful business when the 1980s depression hit. About to lose everything, the store, his family's home, he became severely depressed and began to drink very heavily; he became an alcoholic. From a wonderful family man, he changed into a person no one knew anymore. The bank locked the doors to the store on a Friday, and the next morning, he drove out of the driveway heading south. This devastated his family—wife, children, sisters—relatives, and friends. He would only return home on occasion to attend the children's weddings.

After the last wedding, his wife and family did not hear from him again for a long time. She and his family were heartbroken. Many years passed, and everyone had moved on with their lives with the help of the Lord Jesus Christ.

He continued to work hard, and drank heavily. He searched many churches to "find himself." One day, at a restaurant, a waiter told him he was Orthodox, so he went to visit the waiter's church. When he went to the Orthodox church, he opened the door and saw a full-sized icon of Jesus Christ. There, James fell to his knees, met the Lord Jesus Christ face to face, and it changed his life forever!

After many years, James asked his children if he could come home to visit. They said yes since they still loved him. When he was home, he visited an Orthodox Monastery where he asked the cute girl if she would go there with him.

During the many years that he was away, she had never remarried; took on a job; worked very hard; and built a new home for herself with very much help from the Lord, her family, and friends. She said yes, so they went to the Orthodox Monastery together, a very beautiful and peaceful place. They never left each other's side again and remained in the Orthodox Church. He lived with the love of his life in her peaceful home in the country for twenty more years. James was forgiven.

At the age of eighty-five, James become very ill and passed away peacefully, surrounded by his wife, family, and friends. The funeral was held at the Orthodox Monastery, where he was buried. Praise be to God for the many blessings he and his family had with him in his last twenty years with his wife, his children, five grandchildren, and eleven great-grandchildren.

Reflection of the Reader James Demetrios Crawford

One who knew Jim in his days on the earth will experience his unmistakable voice in the pages of this book. It is as if he is sitting down here with us, reading the words to us. The lines of the text are infused with his personality, his intensity, his love of life in Christ and His holy church; the ink on the paper is transformed into living letters written on his soft heart.

We hear Jim's voice so vividly because he speaks to us from his experience. He is not and never was the type of person simply to pass on abstract information that he had read in a book at some point in time. He loved books, especially the study of the Holy Scriptures together with commentaries on them. And he loved reading the lives of the saints—people who had struggled in this world even as he had and yet who were not held captive to the limitations of the fallenness and brokenness of the arena they inhabited. His words—spoken to us while he was with us and recorded for us here in his repose—arise from the profound healing of his own shattered and disgraced life through the enduring and relentless love of his unyieldingly gentle wife fulfilled in their conversion to and reception into the Orthodox Church.

Indeed, in speaking to us from his own deep and personal experience, Jim stands squarely within the practice prescribed by the Orthodox Church. For there we are exhorted to speak only what we have experienced, what is forged within us on the anvil of our own suffering often, though not always, brought about by our own self-destructive choices battling our own demons, facing the sorrow for the afflictions which we have inflicted on others.

The words that flow from our tongue need to arise from a heart fashioned by God's hands. "A genuine teacher," St. John of Sinai explains, "is he who has received from God the tablet of spiritual knowledge, inscribed by His divine finger" (St. John Climacus, *To the Shepherd* in the Ladder of Divine Ascent, Holy Transfiguration Monastery, Boston, MA, §5 on p. 249).

Speaking from our experience, of course, does not imply infallibility. Not at all. Nor does it suggest some type of moral perfection—a holier than though disposition. It is rather an expression of humility, for it unmasks our pious hypocrisy and opens us to correction. St. Gregory the theologian indicates this when he says, "Discussion of theology is for those who...*at the very least are undergoing purification of body and soul*" (Oration 27.3 emphasis added). Jim speaks neither from abstract ideals nor from a feigned perfectionism but from the current and cleansing operation of the Holy Spirit in his wounded heart.

Jim saw God's presence and abundant generosity in the clouds while he mowed the lawn, in the branches of a tree, in the eyes of a deer, and in the precious body and blood of his Lord and God and Savior, Jesus Christ. But maybe most palpably, the reader, James Demetrios Crawford, experienced God in others and in his service to them. It was in the crucible of the relationships that he came to know God or rather be known by Him, and it is from that very crucible that he speaks to us now.

(From a resident priest of the Orthodox Holy Monastery that Jim attended.)

Introduction

Be at peace, my soul, forever lasting to everlasting approaches. Be at peace, my soul, for the Lord of hosts has called thy name. Be at peace, my soul, the angels have heard, and they rejoice at our approaching. Be still and listen, my soul, for loud is he who refuses to believe and goes into everlasting darkness. Be still, my soul, and contemplate our journey. We shall see he who was crying in the wilderness. Be ye quiet, my soul, keep your lantern lit, and your oil ready for time will run its length, and you will hear the whisper of your Caller. Rejoice and be glad, for your night has finely ended; now the eternal light is forever. It matters not where we have been—on the rocky paths or of shores with the strong surf roaring. In the lush green valleys of great abundance between the mountains high and the mountain paths where some stones lay unturned. What lies beneath those stones we'll never know; those stones have slept in their quiet place since time began; the underside in cold darkness sleeps; the topside in the sunlight warm waits for the passing of each quiet day.

O soul of mine, it all means naught; it all has come and gone. The day has come, and the night prevails as you and I have seen, yet the surf still roars, and the green valley's rocks remain unturned, but you and I must leave. Do not cry; do not weep; our time has just begun. We leave this place just as it was, for time will never end; only you and I will part from that which was to that what it is. Our walk to unknown heights, don't grieve my soul.

By worthless,
Jim L. Crawford

I write this book not for money nor the fame with only a high school education and eighty-four years old. There is only one reason for me to write: for you and the reader and you only.

The person you read about has nothing to hide, no hidden secrets that will in the end overpower you to his way of life. His writings are about his life as it changes through the years—his condition of being addicted to alcohol, leaving his wife and four children, disappearing, and being homeless for days without eating. Passing by rest areas only to stop and dig through the trash barrels to find someone's discarded food. It was pain and suffering from years of running.

Then his life-changing experience of meeting Almighty God, the Creator, before his face. Where after many years of running, the Lord led him back home. Only then the works of the Holy Spirit can this life experience be told in complete simplicity he can tell the way the Holy One worked lovingly to bring his lost soul back from the brink of disaster.

The Word, Jesus Christ, left to sit at the right hand of the Father—the Almighty Creator, and the Holy Spirit left the Father, passing through Christ to come to the earth and seek out the lost, the fallen, and those who love their church and pastor but want and need help in their struggle to understand life, the Bible, and spiritual challenges. The person I write about: I am that person.

In loving memory of James L. Crawford, who passed away at eighty-five years young. Rest in peace, a husband, dad, grandfather and great-grand father, your soul is finally home with Christ and your Father. We love and miss you.

A prayer for the opening of the book. What do you think?

A prayer taken from the book *A Spiritual Psalter* by Saint Ephraim the Syrian, fourth century, translated by Saint Theophan the Recluse to Russian nineteenth century, translated in 1990 by Antonina Janda to English. Published by Saint John of Kronstadt Press.

I write this information for you the reader, because there is so much spiritual information written by men from past centuries available today. Start reading it and you will be amazed at its depth and the inspiration it will create to dig deeper and deeper into our church history. When someone tells you the church was dead through any of the century, it's a lie. The church of Jesus Christ has been and still is a great spiritual beacon of light throughout the world, then and now; the church was not dead, but only the men in it. Nothing has changed. We still have our dead in spirit occupying a seat in the church.

Prayer 115

Because of my extreme corruption, I am unworthy to approach thee, O Lord, and I pray to thee. Up till now and in this very day, with my face ashamed and hung low do I dare to speak to thee, O master of the angels and creator of all things. I, who am earth and dust, a disgrace to men and an insult to mankind; I, who am condemned, all covered with wounds and filled with despondency. How shall I lift my gaze to meet thy grace, O master? How shall I find the boldness to move my impure, polluted tongue? How shall I begin my confession? I, who am wretched, have immeasurably offended thy name and lived wantonly, more so then the prodigal son. In my person have I defiled and injured thine image, for I have not heeded thy commandments.

I know, O Lord, that because of the multitude of my spiritual stains and my impurity, I am not worthy to bear thy holy name, I cannot stand before thee in prayer, I cannot look up and behold the heights of heaven, for I have opened the door to reprehensible desire and surrender to unseemly impulses; and thus have I defiled my poor soul with passions and blackened my soul's garment with the immorality of my will. My whole mind is filled with demonic thoughts. By all deeds and thoughts have I distressed thy grace, and I continue repeatedly to do so. Yet ever do I please and gratify my enemy who wages war against me. My conscience exposes my mind's error; in my heart I cover my face with shame. Before the judgment that awaits me I condemn myself.

Triumphantly do the wanton habits that never leave me drag me along. Ever do I soil myself in the mire of sensuality. I am ever entangled in defiled thoughts; from my youth have I become a vessel corrupting sin, and to this day, though I daily hear of the judgment and of the just deserts to be meted out, I have no will to oppose carnal lust. Ceaselessly do I make myself a prisoner. Woe is me, O Lord; dreadfully have I squandered thy longsuffering patience! Woe is me; how many years have I spent offending thy Holy Spirit! Woe is me; the time of my life has been spent in all manner of vain endeavors!…but, O Lord, do thou not expose me in thy fury; do thou not exhibit my hateful disgraceful deeds in a place of universal shame before all angels and men, to my dishonor and eternal condemnation. According to thy great compassion alone, have mercy on me and cleanse all my sins before the judgment.

Contents

The Wonders of God 15
Chapter 1: Creation 21
Chapter 2: Satan's Control 31
Chapter 3: Sin Nature 37
Chapter 4: The Spiritual Life 42
Chapter 5: Why Christ and the Holy Spirit 56
Chapter 6: The Demon "Avarice" 62
Chapter 7: Common Sense 71
Chapter 8: The Law of Life or Death 84
Chapter 9: The Transfiguration 88
Chapter 10: The Church 102
Chapter 11: Idols 106
Chapter 12: Death 127
Chapter 13: The Soul 152
Chapter 14: Gossiping 165
Chapter 15: Love 169
Chapter 16: The Demonics 187
Conclusion: Repentance 215

The Wonders of God

These writings are true and unexplainable. I lived these experiences and saw with my own eyes, felt with my hands, and will never forget. Many of these things I write about are mine and mine alone. I share these with you the reader because you should know that Christ works through different people in different ways. I will not expound how great a person I am or with pride and vanity expect you to even think such a thing. I have been nothing more than a dumb rock that speaks, a dumb donkey that talks, and a love for Christ that you the reader may not understand. But you will if you find the courage to believe, have a faith that is absolutely impossible to break, and live according to God's will.

"Lord Jesus Christ, Son of God, have mercy on me, a sinner."

Not all prayers are answered, so sometimes we feel left out of God's will. When this happens, do not become discouraged. Even the greatest of saints will talk about this subject, for God has a purpose for your life, and it may not be your desire at the time.

St. Anthony the Great was asked by the wise men of the city, "Why is it that some are healed by prayer and some are not healed?" St. Anthony, who could not read or write, answered, "Go ask God," turned his back on them and went back into his cave.

These experiences took place over a period of thirty years. Many of my prayers were never answered, so who am I to ask "why?" You, the reader, try to understand, if you can, the way forward is sometimes the way backward. Pride will do it every time. I was always too proud to listen to good advice, but I could sure suck up the wrong advice.

One such thing was when I closed the door of my business, threw a whiskey bottle in my car, and drove away. I was that guy who deserts his wife and children, gone for years, and ends up homeless. I walked the roads of life, not only a drunk but a thief, not only a thief and drunkard, but a liar and a conman.

But the Lord Jesus Christ is good and very forgiving. He opened the door to the spirit world, let me see what was happening to my life, and turned my life around. Gone for years, thanks to my wife today, I live in her house, on her land, and through Christ, she forgave me. Years before returning home I had an experience that will stay with me forever. I had come back from lunch. I was in a swampy area next to a bayou, on a two-track road that had a flowing well next to it. It was a place of peace and quiet. As I started to open the door of my truck, a shadow passed over and I looked up to see an osprey. This bird was huge and had a diamondback rattlesnake in its talons. The bird was flying low and slow. He started to circle my truck. Around and around he flew eating the snake at the same time. "Now he is so low," I thought, "he will drop the snake on me." As time passed, this huge bird finished his lunch, tipped his wings at me, and left. And the Lord said, "The snake is dead. I will send you back home. Can I trust you?" Yes, Lord, you can trust me. The Lord said, "Then I will send you home in time," which he did, but not before I was ready. Only through him did I return.

The phone rang and I answered it. It was my neighbor lady down the road. "Mr. Crawford, I'm dying. The doctor gave me two months to live." She was crying and sobbing and asking me to pray for her. "Would you please come and pray for me right now?" I said, "Yes." I started walking to her house.

I had just turned my life over to Christ, now what do I do? How did she know? So many thoughts crossed my mind. Her husband let me in. She sat in the living room in an old overstuffed chair, blanket around her shoulders and across her lap. She explained that she had been a heavy smoker and now she had lung cancer. I put her hand on her chest and mine on top of hers. I started to pray, "In the name of Jesus Christ…" I asked the Lord for a healing and to drive out the spirit of infirmities, heal the damage to the lungs that the cancer had caused, drive out the spirit of pain, and give peace and a long life to this child of God. "Cancer, in the name of Jesus Christ, die and come out of her now." She started choking and spit up black bile. More and more came up. Afterward she lay back in her chair and was at peace. On my way back to the house, I walked in the dark and knew that God answers prayers. This was not my authority over unclean spirits but His and His alone. A feeling of extreme humility came over me, and to this day it has not left. I have been humbled for the rest of my life. My neighbor lady lived two years and passed away in peace after her experience with cancer. Glory be to God.

There was a little boy in our church that had clubfeet. His parents had bought him corrective shoes so he could walk. I had just returned from a Healing Explosion put on in Tampa, Florida, by Charles and Francis Hunter. One night his parents came over to talk with me after their church service. They asked me to please pray for their boy. I said, "Sure," and asked the boy if it was okay with him. He nodded yes. He was six years old and the doctors said he may or may not grow out of his deformity. So he sat down, and I took off his shoes and socks. His sisters and parents, with the pastor of the church, watched. Now, some of the parishioners stayed to watch. I took those little feet in my hands, and in the name of Jesus Christ I asked the Lord to move his bones, correct his little feet, that he would forever be healed. I commanded the feet to become normal, to line up with the leg and ankle bones in the name of Jesus Christ. "By the power of the Holy Spirit, move," I said.

Those little feet moved. They twisted. They turned and then became straight. He put his socks and shoes on and I went home. The next Sunday, his older sister said to me, "My brother can run faster than me." I fell to my knees and cried. The boy came over to me and said, "It's okay, Mr. Crawford." The boy grew up to be a young man and joined the Air Force. I never heard from him again.

For a long time afterward I wondered, "Who am I?"

Lord Jesus Christ, Son of God, have mercy on me, a sinner."

There was a woman that laughed at me during a conversation about spirituality and said, "How could anyone believe such things." In so many words she told me I was a joke and so was spirituality. "How stupid can you be to believe such things?" she said. After the meeting she came over to me and said, "If your Holy Spirit is sent by Christ to help people, then have Christ fix my tail bone. It has been twisted since I was a child. I, to this day, cannot sit in a hard chair without being in pain."

After she insulted me, the old me would have said, "Fix it yourself." But, the new me, the real me, asked her to turn around and put her hand on her tail bone. In a quiet and gentle voice, with my hand on hers, I prayed, "Lord Jesus Christ, in your name, by the power of the Holy Spirit, tail bone, you come in line with the spine; back bone, line up with the hip bone, now, in the name of Jesus Christ, move!" Ever so slowly the tail bone moved and became normal and straight.

She looked at me in utter amazement and said she felt the movement. She started crying.

In her excitement she never did thank the Lord, but the day came later when she did thank Him and did a lot of volunteering at her church.

"Lord Jesus Christ, Son of God, have mercy on me, a sinner."

*****

At the time I was living in Florida, a pastor called me, said he was a pastor of a small church and had a problem at his church. He said there was a spirit in the building and over a period of time had caused so much trouble no one wanted to be left alone in the church. His secretary quit and now the cleaning man quit.

I drove up to meet with the pastor, and he was converted because this morning he was alone in his office typing his sermon for Sunday and the restroom door shut. Being alone in the building, he thought maybe someone had come in and was using the restroom. After time passed he went to the restroom door and knocked. No answer. The stool flushed. After waiting, he knocked again. No answer. He slowly opened the door; no one was there. Water was still running in the stool. He heard the typewriter. He went back to his office and his sermon had been typed over with letters from the typewriter. "What am I supposed to do?" he asked.

A person from my church had come with me and the three of us walked over to the church. First, we shut all the doors and windows. Second, we walked through the church reading Bible verses. Third, I told the unclean spirit to leave in the name of Jesus Christ and now, with holy oil, made the sign of the cross over all of the door jambs and above each window. The back door slammed. The unclean spirit left. I told the pastor, "If he comes back, call me." I never received a call. The pastor's people returned to their jobs. A friend told me, "Things are quiet at the church."

Lord Jesus Christ, Son of God, have mercy on me.

*****

I had been home for a number of years when I was asked to drive out a spirit that had caused trouble for someone very close and dear to my heart. She has had a problem with a man that comes at night. He drags his chains down the hallway to her bedroom. He can hear him coming. She said, "He had many chains hanging from his body, and he moans and groans as he drags his chains." He will not go away but stands in the doorway and looks at her. He keeps her awake and leaves at daylight, dragging his large chains behind him. I said, "Yes, I will come over and tell him to leave. Don't be afraid and don't talk to him."

Our priest gave me this holy oil, and I, a few days later, went to the house with the unclean spirit. I met with the owner (I will not mention her name) and started by telling him to leave in the name of Jesus Christ. Over every door jamb and window trim, I made the sign of the cross—front door, back door, bedroom doors, bathroom doors, downstairs, and through the house. To make sure he or his buddies never return, we took a Q-tip, dipped it in the holy oil, and so making the sign of the cross over the doors and windows, the unclean spirits cannot enter in. O the Cross is like burning coals on their forehead. The unclean spirit that pulled his chains around was never seen again. The cross made with holy oil is there today and will be forever.

Lord Jesus Christ, Son of God, have mercy on me, a sinner.

Chapter 1

Creation

These writings are not for everyone. These things of which are written cannot be changed to fit one's own personal agenda. They are as they are, no assumptions, no guessing, no wondering, and above all, no doubt as to the workings and works that will be forthcoming when these principles are applied. It will be the beginning of a deep confidence unknown to many, caring not for your position or your place in life, but a confidence in who you are.

Going in and coming out will be an experience. Only those committed to a spiritual life can alter their present thought process, therefore changing their natural life. This is the inward look, the deep look into a world unknown to most, unknown to many but yet has been available to all for thousands of years. Because we are made in the image of God our Creator, we are body, soul, and spirit. It makes no difference because of your beliefs—you are still three parts: body (the flesh), soul (the inner self), and the spirit (the supernatural power that infuses or gives us life). Our ability or capacity to relate to God in the spirit is given to us at birth, at the time of conception, but only through the Spirit. Our Lord said, "Before I formed you in the womb, I knew you" (Jeremiah 1:5, New American Standard).

There are many books written on the world of the spirits, but what about the spirit world? Why can a spirit being come into our world and participate in our life and yet we are not able to go into his world? To experience the ability to choose light from darkness, good from evil; to see truth as it actually is, not to be bombarded by lies and deceit, carnality, and corruption as we receive in this world. To keep things simple, let us start form the very beginning.

We want to look into their world, that of the spirit being, the good, the bad, and the ugly. All phases of "Truth" is where we must start from and end at. Because a portion of our self is spirit, then we should be able to see the invisible beings, the spirit itself. No, we cannot. Why? Because of our sin nature. What is my sin nature? It is an invisible covering or a film over our total self. Some of these things are going to be repeated, so don't get bored. Repetition makes for better remembering.

We live in two worlds; one is physical and one is spiritual. We live in both at the same time. We live in the physical, born into it at birth, but the spiritual world is waiting. We cannot yet go there. The two worlds, physical and spiritual, are created by God, the Supreme Being; over all beings in His authority. No one spiritual being or physical being can surpass or become greater than this One Great God the Creator. It does not matter if we believe this or if we deny it; this statement of your Creator is truth, period! If a person does not believe in a God Creator, that is his or her loss. Nothing in that person's life can change because of his or her unwillingness to accept the basic truth. God is your Creator! Pick up your Bible and read Genesis 1:26, "Let us make man in our image, in our likeness."

You or they may deny your Creator, the Creator and Supreme Being, but He does not deny you. He waits. The Creator God is the supreme spiritual being in all the world, and without Him you cannot travel any direction spiritually. You are immobile in physical world—dead in your sin nature. You can have great intelligence, be extremely bright, and have knowledge, but only of the physical world. You and they that do not believe will be locked out, the door shut, the light out, the blackness of the deep will surround you and your spirit. Your spirit will never be able to gain its freedom to live according to its created purpose. This is not an assumption. This is not one person's opinion. This is the truth. This is the difference described between light and darkness; being blind and seeing; hearing and being deaf. If your spirit is not released to make contact with the Creator, then the blindness continues; the sound of the spirit world is completely silent and the pitch of black darkness will prevail until Death makes his call. But make no mistake, do not think for one moment you are going to be free after death. Because one man is lazy and ignorant; or is a hard worker and ignorant; or is responsible or irresponsible; intelligent or illiterate but yet does not believe in his Creator, in his sin nature is open to spiritual attack of the dark side of the spirit world. They will do and live in the unbeliever. They are the familiar spirits we are born with. They control all aspects of your life. They are unknown to you who do not believe. They live in that darkness of the soul itself. They tell the physical self what to do and how to react, how to become proud, vain, arrogant, angry, and despondent. All knowing and yet knowing nothing, staying in denial; irresponsible, obnoxious, and outspoken; shaking their fist at all of us that do not believe as they do. This is certainly not the freedom to do your will but the bondage to do as you are told, which is always their will.

Our sin nature is a covering over our total self. Visualize a covering or haze over your total self; a mist or light covering. Each one of us has our own sin nature or covering over us, some more, some less. Since God was the Creator of the beginning, then at that time man had a speaking, normal relationship with our Supreme Being, God the Father, the Spirit, and All in One. We all know what happened at the time man (Adam) disobeyed the words spoken to him, "Do not eat the fruit from this one particular tree" (Gen. 3:17). Because he did eat or disobey the word, or the law, he falls into a precarious position. Now, he loses his ability to converse with the Lord, his walking and talking; his relationship is fractured, and now his spiritual ability becomes an object, a wall, a disconnect, a total severance with the very one that created him. His spiritual connection has been severed. Now he is told to leave the environment of the spiritual world and be forced out into the physical world. Now his hands are put to the ground, his feet put to the ground, his physical self now is grounded in the environment of the physical world. For the first time, a world of evil and sinfulness surrounds him. Now his freedom of expression with God is destroyed. His Father now moves away from him because of his sin nature. Now the sin nature covers him totally for the first time.

In the spiritual world, they are who they are. They have no choice of being what they want to be. The spirit of fear is a being. He, this being, this demon, this voice who speaks to us at his choosing, cannot be the spirit of pride. He, the demonic spirit called pride, cannot be anyone else. They are who they are as individuals, not as a mist or a cloud, all being the same spirit or one gigantic self. Each one has his own identity. The spirit of anger cannot be fear or pride, yet they call to each other and work in conjunction or side by side with each other continually. They all are under the full authority of Satan, the one who wants to be God; the one who wants full control over all things created, spiritual and physical. Now this is what Adam is faced with—a nature that welcomes evil and enjoys sinfulness.

He, Satan, now brings his unclean spirits into man's life because man obeyed Satan and disobeyed God. Satan now has control of part of man's self, not all of man's self but part of man's self. Now Satan becomes the relationship with man; God's relationship has been stolen or hijacked. In the world of the spirits, there is no option for disobedience. If you lived there, you would obey one of the two voices: God the Father, Creator of truth, or Satan, the liar. There is no other choice. Take your pick. Satan is the most disobedient of all that are known. Satan disobeyed God the Almighty and was thrown out of God's presence. Now, the spirit of Satan lives in the lower world, a world of complete darkness. This disobedience is not hard to describe—the disobedience toward God. One of the angels to fall with Satan is disobedience. Now, he the being is Satan's tool to disrupt the laws of God's profound place he has for us. As spoken to describe "truth" in God's time of creation, stop and think! Snow does not burn! This is God's created "truth or spiritual law," like it or not, it is as it is! "Truth" is as it is!

Man does not have wings; he by his own physical self cannot fly. We were not created to stay suspended in the air or walk through fire without being burned. All things created will do only as they are created for. Nothing more, nothing less! The spirit is absolute. Be he from the darkness on the evil side or from the light and its awesome exhilaration on the side of God the Creator. Both sides of this spirit world have an agenda. Both are after the person's soul. Nothing can deviate this agenda. Satan, in his hate for God, will take the soul down into his pit and will torment the spirit of that person forever. We are made in the image of God of whom he hates. God will take the soul and spirit up into His kingdom because of his great love for each man, woman, and child. No distinctions, no reservations, no contemplating on the who is or who is not what position they hold or have held while on Earth.

Satan's hate for God shows in the hate people have for God and God's kingdom in that world. Hate, anger, confusion, depression, and all his ability to lie and deceive mankind are tools to capture our souls. God's love for mankind shows through his compassion, forgiveness, sensitivity, peace, suffering, prosperity and all the virtues, wisdom, love, and a relationship of a greater kind than anything known to man.

Two absolutes in one world, so it has been for thousands of years. The spirit world has not changed. God's absolutes are the same today as they were when He created the world. This is why God said, "I am the same yesterday, today and forever" (Heb. 13:8). I will call them absolutes and not laws because a law strikes a feeling in our inner self that wants for some of us to defy it or try to ignore it or just plain displace it out of our lives. A law can be changed at some time or place; a law given to man by man will be broken at some time, more sooner than later. No matter what the repercussion or penalty might be, we see this continually in our society and daily life. Someone has to reason it out or has to think about it. If it fits into my life today, it's okay; if it doesn't fit into my life today, then let's just ignore it. This is our physical world today. We have laws and we have options. Different places in the world have different laws, different countries, different penalties for those who violate the law.

We have options to move out of this country because we don't like the people or the laws. Let us move over to another place where we can have greater freedom and more options. This is our physical world simply put. The spirit world is absolute; two options, no changes, it is as it has been forever. One option we have is our belief in God; the other is belief in the world.

Some find a dead church because there is no obedience there. Are people happy in a dead church? Some are. They have on their mind only one thing: an uninterrupted life, a physical life each day that will satisfy the limited needs in their life as long as it lasts. It is their option; remember, in your beginning at your birth! You are a physical body with a soul and spirit, all in one. This is extremely important that you never should forget who you are and how you were made. No options! In your beginning, how you were born, where you were born., did you have a parent or you didn't have parents, one parent or no parent, abused or not abused, believing in God or if you are godless. It makes no difference whatsoever, you do not have an option or a choice; you are who you are. Period! Like it or not! You are chained to your sin nature forever unless you spiritually break free!

Our society has brought all of this guilt upon us, that we should be someone else. We should be doing better; or we can't get out of this rut; my parents are at fault; my dad's fault, he drinks; my mother wasn't there when I needed her the most; I could have done better if I had money; I'm too poor; I'm not going to leave my soft secure safe place to go out and help someone; I made this all by myself and I'm not going to share it with anyone. I don't like myself! I hate myself! On and on and on! No matter how rich or how poor. Because you are the member of the dead church or don't believe at all makes no difference. Because you think you are filled with the Holy Spirit and are holy and righteous.

Because you have a beautiful church and a good life, a good life with no church; a bad life in a good church or a bad life with no church. It makes no difference. Stop being critical of yourself and quit denying your responsibility for your own being. You are who you are! Period! You are still physical, soulish, and spiritual, no matter what your circumstances. Start today to admit to yourself you are a created being made in three parts: the physical body, the soul, the spirit; living in you that is the very connecting rod between you and the Lord. Like it or not, believe it or not, this is an absolute. Born into this world, born naked and made in God's image, physical, soulful, and spiritual. Admit to yourself who you are!

Born with an invisible film surrounding us, our sin nature, it comes with us in the package. Some have a darker thicker film, some have a lighter film, some medium or some depending on God's grace, a film brighter and thinner than most. Now visualize this spiritual absolute. This must be understood before we can proceed. Before we can go further into this realm of thinking about entering the world of the spirit, visualize an egg. Stand it on end, look at it as yourself. This is who you are. I don't care about your education, how smart you are, stop thinking about how simple and stupid this is for that voice comes from the pit. Believe it or not, simplicity is a powerful tool in our spiritual warfare. Simplicity is the breastplate of our armor against evil. The egg now stands on end.

The shell is our physical body; it protects the inner workings. The mind belongs to the physical and is your outer voice. The egg white, as you visualize the inner egg, is your soul, your consciousness in who you are. This is your inner voice. The egg yolk is your spirit. It cannot be separated from your soul and no more than the egg white and yoke can be separated, both are joined together for a blending of greater strength; this is in its natural form. The best taste of the whole egg is the yolk when it is prepared properly. The egg white surrounds the yolk, and whether we fry it or scramble it, both are intertwined. But to boil the egg in hot water, it separates the white of the egg from the yolk and the shell is peeled off from the white of the egg. It can be separated with effort and a proper procedure. This example is the same as the workings of the physical. Our sin nature is the egg shell, the soul is the egg white, the yoke our spirit, the yoke being the sweetest most inner part of the egg.

Our Lord said, "I knew you before you were conceived" (Jer. 1:5). How does He know us? How does he know each individual person? Because we are born with a spirit in us, your spirit is the real you, the true you. God knows every spirit being in every child ever born. Throughout the Old Testament, God knew those that were against Him and knew those that were for Him. He, the Creator,

God, looks at your spirit and your soul. From the time of Adam to this very day, nothing has changed in the world of the spirits. Your physical self is the acting out of who we think we should be. Satan still tries to capture the soul and spirit of each of us. Take us to the pit; separate us from our Creator. How angry would you be at your children if they did not obey your command to stay in the yard at your house, don't go out in the street and play, don't go down the street to the unrighteous neighbor's house and spend all your time with them, stay close to me so that you won't become lost in this crowded place. We have all heard these commands from our parents and adults over us. They were looking out for our well-being. Again and again we hear these commands as years go by. Some pay attention, others do not; some never feel the warmth that security brings as they are intent on disobedience; some never hear the voice at all they are left to roam the streets alone, doomed to total failure. But we do have a choice, for better or for worse.

It is an absolute; physical change does not bring us a spiritual change. But spiritual change brings us physical change.

Depending on our shell, our sin nature that covers our soul and spirit, we can or cannot obey the word of God our Creator. Depending on our family's past, our genealogy, our own wants and needs, we cannot determine that thickness of our shell that governs our being. The invisible covering is only seen by and in the spirit world. They, the spirits, see a light shining through the shell or they see total darkness inside. By your soulish commitment to change spiritually, you can break the shell of your sin nature and be free.

The soul and spirit of our birth becomes locked inside our sin nature and cannot have any communication with the heavenly spirit it so much longs for, the very world it was created for. The evil world of the spirit realm has complete control over our being at the time of our birth. For some of us, at no time in our life is this evil authority ever questioned. It is our willingness to live this way forever, in the sinful pleasures of the physical world; work, play, cry, hurt, party, and on and on. I owe it to myself to enjoy my life; let's all party down! Don't tell me about the spiritual laws; don't tell me about spiritual commandments. I know all about those things. Ridiculous, these religious bigots! A bunch of hypocrites! Other of us find the security of spiritual laws questioning; are these things real; do they exist; do they affect our physical lives? How do they affect us if they are the laws that should be followed? I want a reason to believe; I want to know for sure before I commit myself to these things. Some of us are known very early in life to accept the spiritual laws as part of the fullness of life and would never ever feel comfortable in the world of evil and daily sinfulness that we may call "life in general." But yet others deny the fact that they have problems brought on by their very own sinful nature.

Have you ever heard this said? I'm not a sinner; I'm not doing anything wrong. I stay home and take care of my house and my children, my wife, my husband, my mother, my father, and my work. I work hard every day; I try to be good; I am a good person; I pay my bills; I have things nice: a home, cars, and some money. I earned every bit of it; all of this is mine, and don't think for one minute it isn't! Have we heard the words before, "No, God never gave me a thing, I made it by myself"? The words spoken about spiritual laws concerning our Lord Jesus Christ infuriates some people, depending on their belief. These words bounce off our sin nature/our shell) like darts bouncing off a heavy metal dart board. Some religious people continue to throw their darts against the metal dart board of other people's sin nature, and we ask ourselves, why would you throw a dart at a metal dart board, knowing it will never stick? They hope someday the religious words will stick to what they call "that unrighteous person," to put it mildly. Isaiah chapter 29 verse 13, "These people honor me with their lips but their heart is far from me." The very person that professes to be so righteous and preach their religion is sometimes the very person who keeps his soul and spirit in chains, never breaking the thick shell of his own sin nature.

In the ancient writings of the early church, the saint said of this particular religious motivation: "to take the word of God to an unbeliever and try to humiliate him or her into believing by confronting them with scriptures is like putting a fine gold necklace around a pig's neck." We cannot break the covering of our sin nature by words alone. The shell of the egg cannot be cracked or broken by speaking to the egg. We know that! Set a boiled egg on the table and tell it to crack or tell it to break. Certainly, it is a waste of time and energy.

Adam, after falling, gave Satan the authority to take control of our soul and spirit by the disobedience to the word of his Creator Father God. Before Adam/man disobeyed God's word, God's spiritual command was, "don't violate this spiritual law; do not take into yourself the sweetness of disobedience." Visualize a spirit being as an object, a person or thing, whatever or however, but separate it from other beings, each spirit being has a job to fulfill. Each has his own personality.

Enough said. We will look into their world later on in the future chapters. It is very important to remember one thing, we never call the Holy Spirit "It," for He is God and will always be acknowledged as "He," the Spirit of God. Because "He" is yours and mine. He is our very lifeline that makes us change spiritually. In later chapters He, the Holy One, will be explained in more detail.

Chapter 2
Satan's Control

Now Satan calls Disobedience to him and says I will entice Adam's wife Eve by whispering these lies to her. He explains the procedure to Disobedience, so Disobedience now comes to Eve as a feeling; we all know that feeling when we know we are doing the wrong thing, coming against what we know we should do. Finding a reason for our disobedience is just common knowledge justified by excuses and reasoning. Eve listens to Satan's voice, now out comes a lying spirit. He has been called upon to enter into the attack. Under the feeling of excitement caused by Satan's voice in Eve's being, the lying spirit enters in, and now Eve has begun to let herself fall into the hands of the evilness that Satan has surrounded us with. The excitement of evil! This excitement of evilness has been around that long; since our creation and thousands of years before. Satan'shate for mankind is greater than any hate except his total hate of God himself. Satan's hate of your spirit is beyond knowing. To capture your soul and spirit is the real objective, the only objective, his greatest accomplishment known in this world since Adam and Eve to this day. This very day you should read these words is the very day Satan is looking at you to persuade you to sin; satisfying your sin nature, giving in to your temptations called "bad habits." These things now open the door for his demons to control your whole physical being, your soul and your complete self, your spiritual being. Now Satan can claim you for himself, and his hate for you now becomes the open obsession for your future, with him, in his world. The pit of everlasting pain and fear, darkness, and the sickening stench of burning souls, the screams of the spirits burning in the fire of everlasting torment. Our soul cannot escape; his wrath is beyond human imagination.

Where are the wise men of our times? Where are the theologians, great or small, of our times? The ones that speak long words and are so intellectual that they cannot tell us in a simple and understandable way how to save our soul and spirit from this spirit world Satan controls. A man once said, "Some intellectuals do not have enough common sense to park a bike straight." Why don't they explain the workings of the spirit world that controls our very being every day of our life? We need someone to take us to the spirit world to show us why and how and what we should do to correct our lives by disciplining our flesh. Stop our passions from dictating our everyday performance in a world today that expects us to act this way or that way, to be successful in our so-called society.

Satan controls our society; God controls the Earth. Why are the laws of society unwritten? They conform to Satan's plan for our sin nature to slide us gently down the tube of destruction as our flesh loves every hour of its joy that we find in sinfulness. Look at your Bible, if you have one, Luke Chapter 1, verses 39, 40, and 41, "But the Lord said, 'to him, now you Pharisees clean the outside of the cup and of the platter, but inside of you, you are full of robbery and wickedness.'"

Be careful of the strong message being sent out of the church in these last years. Many of our pastors cry "send me your money and I will send you great abundance." There will be scriptures flowing from his lips as he waits for his abundance to arrive. Be careful; be alert; be vigilant, for many of these so-called great men of God can't park a bike straight. That is how incapable they are if you were to go any deeper than their mind. Some are spiritual-minded, some are not! Is the mind our total governing criteria? That is what Satan wants us to think and believe; that is what we all believe if we know not Christ. By not knowing Christ, the mind will not comprehend the scriptures, spiritual words and sayings, spiritual phenomena and miracles, and it will always be subject to its limited worldly knowledge of such things.

As we look around at people in our lives, we see some that even become very angry when we speak or try to understand anything spiritual. Their mind says, "Don't listen to this garbage talk, life has enough problems." "What we do in our walk of life is strictly our choice. and anything I have accomplished is of my own works; God is too busy elsewhere." Ask them, how did you get where you are today, your wealth, your home, your family? If they start with the words "I am," then you know there could be a problem with Vanity, a spirit straight out of the pit. There is only one "I am," and never forget this as we begin our spiritual walk "I AM THE GREAT I AM" spoken by God Almighty many times in the Old Testament. Very simple, so simple it is overlooked and will be passed by continually. He, Pride and he, Vanity hate to hear these words because it causes them to shake and tremble and in the end, have to fall away from that person or person's realm they live in. Whatever you have accomplished or want to accomplish, whatever you want to change or see changed, you must remember God's word, "I am the Great I am," and He governs all things in your life. You cannot ever make one change of one circumstance without Him. Christian or non-Christian, agnostic, unbeliever, Satan worshiper, or whatever we call ourselves, He, the Lord God Almighty, controls all things visible and invisible. Nothing moves on this Earth without His knowing and observance. This is step no. 1 in our preparation to enter the world of the spirit. In our observance of their world, "the world of the spirits," we should take time to prepare our soul and spirit to make this journey. Luke chapter 12 verse 7 states, "The Lord said 'indeed the very hairs of your head are numbered. Do not fear,'" and verse 31, "But seek His kingdom and all things will be given to you."

As we have just talked about, the mind being in full control at all times of our life, or so Satan would have us believe, this is not true; you are not your mind. It doesn't matter that some people of great knowledge will call these writings ignorance and illusions, written by the uneducated and unlearned. If you have tried their way, the way of the world and have found the laws of society have not worked to make a change in your life or gave you a perspective with an absolute foundation, then maybe you may want to read on. Just to satisfy your curiosity or is there a knowing that must be satisfied. In the name of the Father and of the Son and of the Holy Spirit. Amen. "For though ye have ten thousand instructors in Christ, yet ye have not many fathers" (l Cor. 4:15). Why?

We cannot go any further until we settle our knowing of who we are. Who am I and why am I and where am I? Remember we said we are body, soul, and spirit; remember the egg. The hard shell is the flesh, controlled by the mind. Our sinful nature is in full control of the mind-body combination.

At any time, our sin nature can and will control the mind to control the body or will control the body to control the mind. That is why the person who says from his or her heart, "I am in full control of my life, I am the maker and supplier of my destiny," is so tempted by the spirit of pride, only to be blindsided by Vanity and now walks through their life blind to all spiritual knowledge and falls off course. They call these habits or just normal or natural ways of our life. Expect it, there is nothing you or I can do about it. What are the unclean spirits or demons or fallen angels, any spirits of the lower pit, doing in our life, tempting us, forming habits we will live with for a lifetime? We do not have a clue. When Adam accepted the temptation by the spirit of evil, he severed the spiritual wire to God the Father; God Almighty; the Father of my Lord, Jesus Christ. And he, Adam, fell, his death in sin fell upon us.

The mind and body have been under the control of Satan's presence ever since, to this very moment.

At no time can you break away or break out of this spiritual realm by yourself. Never, never, never!

Snow does not burn, an absolute, so this is an absolute. The mind and body will forever be in the darkness of the authority of the fallen one, Satan, and the followers that fell with him. So is the state of this person forever. No matter how poor or rich he may be, no matter how beautiful she is or how rich and glorious they live or how they paint themselves with beauty to hide their shallow inner self.

> They in their darkness gropeth. And thou shalt grope at noonday, as the blind gropeth in dark-

ness and thou shalt not prosper in thy ways: and thou shalt be only oppressed and spoiled evermore and no man shall save thee. (Deut. 28:29)

The Lord God, absolute controller of all things and all people, has said, "They shall be spiritually blind, even in broad daylight"; they cannot see the light or knowledge of His (the Lord's world) kingdom. And they will not prosper in their ways, meaning they will never be happy with their own property. No matter how rich you become, unless you are a child of His, you will be unhappy/despondent, always looking elsewhere for your pleasures. Unless your spirit is free and your soul satisfied by God's presence, you will not prosper spiritually. Your spoiled spiritual life is like rotting spoiled food, and your oppression is from your familiar unclean spirits that pound you and hound you where you cannot and will not find peace. There is not one place on Earth where you can find peace and spiritual contentment without your Father God Almighty. Society's world cannot offer you this place because as long as we deny our spiritual relationship with God Almighty, we are having a relationship with the enemies of the very God that created us. It is very common for the unbeliever to live his or her life in what looks like a good life; but underneath is what the Lord sees; He ignores the top dressing and looks to see who is inside. "Ye are of your father the Devil and the lusts of your father ye will do" (John 8:44). Why do we do this?

If we are not of God the Creator, then we will be with the ruler of darkness. Because we are not free from our sinful nature and cannot free ourselves, we are at the mercy of the lower realm; darkness will prevail. Your spirit stays locked inside of your shell, the sin nature. "He that is of God heareth God's word, ye therefore hear them not, because ye are not of God" (John 8:47). Why?

Who came first, God or the Church? In knowing the church, it means nothing because we must know God first. Many people do not want to hear this and will deny its truth. They come to church and work at the church because this is a good sociable detachment from the world, from stress and job-related boredom. Yet, they know not God. Because the flesh has authority over the spirit and the soul, there will be no contact with the Lord. Our sin nature prohibits this contact while the flesh enjoys the sinfulness that surrounds it. This is the person's choice. Do we live with our flesh in control or do we live with the soul and spirit free, having given the spirit and soul the authority over the flesh? Meanwhile, Satan has full control over our sin nature and at any time sends his unclean spirits to control the flesh; therefore, the flesh does Satan's work at any given moment.

The demonic comes, wipes his finger across the man's brain, and the flesh is on fire from the touch.

"The thrill of being high." When we read about "the lusts of our father and his lusts we will do," this is the meaning of this very Scripture. This means we will do whatever is told to us by the evil one, since we do not fully and totally give our self to Christ, then we will have a father who permits us to enjoy his sin nature, and so if we do not understand sin or sinfulness, we do it as a part of our life—normal day-to-day struggling.

CHAPTER 3
Sin Nature

There was a very knowledgeable Christian pastor on national TV one night. The journalist who is a Christian asked the pastor, "What is sin?" After some hesitation and pausing to contemplate, the pastor starts speaking about the cross, Christ crucified, to deliver us from our sinfulness. Cannot the pastor explain sin? Why, when thousands of people watch and wait for someone to explain something so simple but yet has so powerful a hold on their lives, "What is sin?" Many volumes have been written on this subject, long and deep verbalization, great thinkers, many ideas and explanations. But since I am simpleminded and do not have a formal education; since we are talking spiritual and worldly; since sin is nothing more than our life of disobedience of God's word, it reads for a very simple explanation. The complicated part of sin is if you deny it. And, be alert, listen; who just jumped up and said in your mind "not me," what feeling do you recognize coming over you when you read these words about sinfulness? Even those whose love for Christ is so great they gave up their life for Him must fight this same feeling when asked about sin. Have you heard, "Who me, I am not a sinner"? It is not complicated, just deny it and go on with your life, it's that simple. Is it that simple? Can we deny a way of life? Sure. Why not? I was in a denying life for fifty-some years. So what made me; what makes many of us, young and old, want to change? There is a Scripture in your Bible in the Old Testament, "Be still and know that I am God" (Ps. 116:10). Many of our denominations in Christian churches have their favorite verses from the Bible. Let us not confuse the importance of any one verse, "Be still and know that I am God." What does this have to do with sin, our sin nature, our sinful life, or our denial of sin in our life? To deny God's existence is the denial of His spiritual laws totally, and to deny and disobey the spiritual ordinances, His commandments, His covenant with us, which is His contract with us to keep us free and safe, this is sin. This is sinfulness.

Remember our conversation in previous chapters, there will be those who will question my ability in the meaning of these Scriptures. One way to know the truth is in simplicity; keep it simple and all will understand its meaning. If the explanation of a verse or Scripture is so complicated, it leaves me numb, then the explainer or teacher is spinning yarn, trying to baffle us with their brilliance. We are not interested with brilliance, we want truth, the truth, the freedom from our old habits, addictions, way of life, or to finally want to be who I am; change my life and simply be me. This change cannot be made—never, ever. No one on this Earth can change you or change themselves without knowing truth, the Lord Jesus Christ. Truth cannot be found without stillness, be still, be quiet, stop, be only with *you*. If you cannot shut off your TV, radio, telephone, and all other material things, then you know one thing for sure; you are locked into a world too busy to make changes. It is a spiritual effort to be still, to be quiet, to stop the spinning, to contemplate on change. You must be like the cat with a mouse: don't let go. "But it drives me crazy to be still, I hate quiet, I must have noise of some kind." Have you ever heard that before? Is this your life—turn on the radio, music, football, sports, talk radio, on and on? So we enjoy noise, these things are okay, but not for twenty-four hours, seven days continuous pounding that is unmerciful to our spiritual life.

Truth cannot be found here; truth cannot live in that environment; reasoning and denial live there, confusion and the spirits of doubt and lust, carnality, addiction, and above all else, gluttony lives in the environment of noise, spinning, rushing here, hurry there, get this kid over there, put this kid over here, put this or that worldly agenda first.

Spiritual time? Come on, get real, better yet, go get lost; I'm too busy and I'll catch up later on, maybe someday, but not today, and on and on and on. This is when passion controls our life. So you are making a spiritual effort to follow the way of the world. The world's way is natural to our sinful nature. Being busy with our life is normal, so how can it be sinful? "He who is not with me is against me" (Luke 11:23). Does this make any sense at all? If you are not with him in your daily life, then the other guy is in control and he, "the other guy," is against God's principles.

Human nature since Adam is a life without spiritual guidance from your God. Father the Creator who brought you into this world to worship Him and to be secure under His great umbrella of faith, truth, peace, love, kindness, patience, and perseverance under all circumstances and situations life will confront us with. So to fall away from our spiritual truth, His ever-knowing umbrella of protection for our life is left open only for us to crawl out from underneath it and expose ourselves to the spiritual sinful nature of the natural life, which, in reality, what we have done is to fall under the umbrella of the demonic world and its temptations; full of joyful expectation which bring a covering for delusion, doubt, conflicting adversities, and compound iniquities.

A house full of unclean spirits coming in new to control the life of this person. Read Luke 11:24–26 in your Bible. Christ is speaking in Luke 11:24:

> When an evil spirit comes out of a man it goes through places seeking rest and it does not find it. Then it says "I will return to the house I left." When it arrives it finds the house swept clean and put in order. Then it goes and takes seven other spirits more wicked than itself, and they go in and live there. And the final condition of that man is worse than the first.

We use the Book of Luke because in these particular circumstances, the writings pertain to our subject matter. We will look at other books and verses in the Bible as time progresses. Luke 11:24 says, "when the unclean spirit goes out of a man." The Lord Jesus Christ is speaking; no higher spiritual authority is there throughout the universe, the world, or outer space. There is not many man or woman or child that can tell you spiritual laws and how the world they live in operates and functions. And above all else, how they, the "spirits," affect us in our daily lives, in our sinful nature, in our urge to change, and finally, in making a change in our life. How will we operate and function as the evil spirit in us has, for the present time, authority over our flesh, our sinful nature?

Now we return to the unclean spirit going out again. If the unclean spirit goes out, then it must be he was in the man, living in the person. I'm sure you understand he had to be in there before he could come out. What's he doing in there anyway? How did he get in? How does a spirit enter into a person and then, above all else, set up shop, make a house, and live in comfort while the man knows nothing about the unclean spirit's presence.

Is this the exception or is it normal? It's normal. Now there are people who will tear their hair out denying any spirit of any kind lives in them. We understand. But we are looking to make some changes in our life and we are looking closely at all aspects. Leave no stone unturned. This is my life, this is the most important profound decision made in my lifetime. I want to know the truth.

In later chapters we will talk about how they, the unclean spirits, enter in. For now we will continue with the Lord's explanation of the spirits exist.

If "it," the spirit, is unclean, it means he is from the lower pit, or darkness, or demonic environment.

Unclean means he is sinful by nature and will trash your house for you. What's that mean? That means it comes into your spiritual house that is inside of every human on earth. Remember the three parts: the physical, the spiritual, and the soul. It, the unclean, has made its home in our spiritual nature and brings with it a feeling. Maybe you don't recognize it, but it's there; remember one thing more about this spirit world. Every evil spirit, unclean spirit and familiar spirit, has its own feeling, its own job, its own attitude, and is connected with all others of its evil kind, some worse than others.

So "it," the unclean spirit, has made problems for this man, which they all do, and the Lord says the unclean spirit went out of the man into waterless places; meaning out into the air, the environment, not into dirt, animal, trees, or any other human. This man had to have an association with spiritual discipline to expel the spirit. He must have wanted to break a bad habit, try to change his ways of living, but to be permanent, this can only be done by Christ himself. For us it's prayer, faith, and discipline. In the Lord's explanation, He says the unclean spirit left, went into waterless places looking to rest. It's looking for a warm place to hide. It is weak and cold, and it now returns to its old hiding place, looking inside the man and sees that his old room is empty.

Why is it empty? What empty room do you have inside you? Luke 11, verse 25 says it's swept clean and put in order. The man's life at this point is going quite well. He rid himself of some bad habits and feels good about himself and his being is confident and proud about this newfound freedom. But not for long. Disaster cometh.

Remember when we made some decisions and thought we were on the road to utopia, we were great then, and our decisions were what we called "masterful." When all I needed was "me," it was all about "me." Sure I went to church, sat in the back pew, and spent my time teaching Sunday school and doing community work. But deep inside of me I said to myself, "This is my place, no one can see me here. I'm saving this place for me. No one, no one knows who I really am, but me." Be careful, your spiritual room is swept clean and only you alone can make this choice, fill it with the spirit of the Lord God, the Holy One, or it will be filled with the unclean spirit that left, but it returned with seven more stronger spirits than itself; now devastation comes and last for years. Can you make sense of what has happened here? Undetected, the unclean spirit can come and go without being detected or identified. This is because we, in our physical nature, are spiritually blind. Our makeup, our physical makeup, all parts of our body, our flesh function together to give us life, to work, play, and live according to our personal choice or according to circumstances given us. Now without spiritual knowledge, we do not understand our own feelings. Since we have covered lightly the physical, let's look at our spiritual makeup. The unseen controlling factor in our life.

Chapter 4
The Spiritual Life

This takes place deep within us. For some of us it's so deep we cannot or will not recognize its existence, but it's there. Test it, read your Bible. God made this a part of you, like it or not; you are stuck with a spiritual makeup, a spiritual room, a place where only spiritual phenomenon take place, good, bad, or ugly. But it takes place, and you know it or don't know it. Seen or unseen. Known or unknown. This is that place the Lord Jesus Christ talked about as the unclean one exited and returned with seven more worse than itself. The reason it brought its buddies back with it was because it was weak and could not withstand the cleaning up in the man's life. So it says this time when I go back in there, I'll have some helpers, big guys, extra tough dudes, then I know I'll be safe for a long time. And the man's life becomes worse than ever before.

For some people the spiritual makeup, the unseen room of spiritual presence is very close to the surface of their everyday life and we see in them a different aspect, either more loving and kind or more evil and demonic. A Christian with the Holy Spirit living in him or her stands looking at a person with an unclean or evil spirit living in them and says, "There is something about that person that makes my skin crawl my hair wants to stand on end." The person with the evil spirits stands looking at the persons with the God spirit living in them and he says, "I don't like those people, I'm not comfortable around them. They are so self-righteous they make me sick." To put it mildly.

Depending on who is living in us in that room or house, their authority controls our very life and existence. They press the button, we respond. The Lord called it the Spirit's house, so shall we from this time on. We have our physical house, our spiritual house within the body and our soulish or consciousness area in that same house. The soul and the spirit are as one.

So as we return to stillness, return to our starting line that we walked away from to get some info on our inner self. Now stillness in a person's life has and will bring about change, in our thinking and living. It gives us time to contemplate, meditate, make decisions crucial to our everyday life, and above all, makes us more aware of what is happening in our life, future, present, and past. Saint John Climacus in *The Ladder of Divine Ascent* on spiritual beings has a good description of our minds when we are overwrought with constant noise, plans that don't materialize, people we depend on don't come through as planned, hardships and suffering that appear but not planned for, on and on.

He says our mind is "sometimes like a greedy kitchen dog addicted to barking"; we must change this to a lover of chastity and watchfulness. This will be a good fight, hard and close, but fight we must to regain our right to obtain a firm foundation to rebuild and reconstruct the house of who we are, of who we will be, want to be, and can be.

This is our spiritual battle, our war within ourselves. No one has to know, no one has to be your counselor and confirm and reconfirm your decision. In your quiet time, go for a walk, sit in the park, walk in the woods, sit in your backyard, watch nature on a country road sitting in your car, no radio, no smoking, no newspaper, no, no, no, no talking only to yourself. Is your mind full of things you should do, be doing, sure it is. Let the dog bark and he'll wear you out. Your mind keeps on running. Take your Bible with you. Read it, even if you don't understand a word of it or put everyone to bed and read the Scriptures. Stillness, now Scriptures. "I don't do stillness and I sure don't do the Bible! Give me a break! Take your book and stick it in your ear. I'm going to go on with my life and take whatever comes." These words are said over and over again. In the very beginning, it is certain with great labor we will begin our renunciation of the world and its sinful nature and our bad habits. What you gain from stillness and the Scriptures are virtues.

Virtues come from the truth being brought to you through the Spirit. The Holy One of God who stands waiting for you to begin your journey. Time means nothing to Him; he waits for you to make your choice. The barking dog or peace, faith, love, confidence, respect, and above all, the Spirit that drives all others out of your spiritual house, cleans it up, organizes it, and puts it in order. The Holy One. You and I have an opportunity to acquire the only being in the universe that can change our life, the Holy Spirit. At no time in the history of mankind has there ever been a spiritual time as now.

Stop and think!

No other human can change your life, only you; your lifestyle, or the way of living can change. You who you are cannot change, unless you make a choice.

The unclean spirits that live in us must go and be replaced with the Holy One, the Spirit of God. With Him, now your house is occupied, and when the unclean spirit comes back after he has left he can bring as many tough guys, bad dudes, evil doers as he wants, but he cannot enter in, because your house is not empty; it is occupied by the highest spiritual authority known in this world and it is His world, the world of the Holy Spirit. Our Lord Jesus Christ said, "I must leave you but I will send the Holy Spirit to help you," and our Lord also said, "The Holy Spirit will be poured out on all mankind." He makes no exceptions. We who are addicts, alcoholics, lusting after money, fame, women, men from the highest to the lowest, nonbelievers, God haters, murderers, haters of all people and places, like raging beasts they kill and destroy for their own pleasure. The Holy Spirit is available to all mankind.

Why did the Lord Jesus Christ look down from the cross and say, "Father, forgive them for they know not what they do!" Only God knows who was in the spiritual house of each man that came to condemn Christ. But whatever spirit it was led the men to hate Christ and those who followed Him. Christ knew the spirits, "Read your Bible," they talked to Him. He talked to them, but not for very long. Mostly he commanded them. No formal conversations as we are accustomed to. He saw the spirits of murder, lies, contempt, gluttony, insensibility (meaning dead souls), cowardice, vain glory, pride, and passion. They, the evil ones, sat and looked at Him, and in their rage and hate of Him, they urged the men whom they controlled, as they still do, to kill and destroy. Still today they punish us; mankind suffers under their authority over the world.

    We will look at this in more detail in later chapters. But because of those that doubt the Spirit has authority over us, let us look again to the Scriptures for detail that support this conclusion. Take your Bible, open it to 1 Kings chapter 22 verse 19. Micah, the prophet of God, is speaking to the king of Israel, Ahab. Now beware! Don't assume these prophets are just ordinary men. The king and his court and the king's people in the established lesser courts also think as the king thinks. We as people vote for our king or president, as we call him. We are now judged with those who we think as he thinks. The ungodly will vote for an ungodly candidate, the Christian votes for a godly man, and the religious undisciplined will vote for a religious make believe, a person who carries a Bible but is an immoral hypocrite. To put the setting in perspective, first we must know that King Ahab is king or ruler over all of Israel at that time. King Ahab wants to go to war to acquire more land for Israel. So he is asking all his court, should I go to war? In those days the king's court was shared by false prophets who think and in speaking, stay in line with the king's wants and needs. So when asked, "Should I go to war?" the king's false prophets say in 1 Kings chapter 22 verse 12, "the Lord will give it into the king's hands." Just what the king wants to hear. None of these men speak with honesty and truth, none carry the Holy Spirit, have a spiritual connection needed to proclaim the actual function and to do His "the Lord's will" as He wants it done. To do His will, we must have a spiritual connection to His voice, His understanding to gain His knowledge and wisdom, to be able to discipline oneself to follow in His footsteps as He leads us through our life. According to His will, not our will.

    Now Micah, God's prophet, speaks to the king when asked, "Should I go to war?" In verse 15 Micah speaks to the king, and being facetious, Micah says, "the Lord will give it into the king's hand." He speaks the same message as the worldly prophets in the king's court because he knows the king is not going to listen to the truth of God's word. He only wants to hear what he, the king, wants to hear and see. Does this remind you of someone, someone you know quite well? It's all about me.

Do we contemplate about our major or minor decisions, do we pray about them with an open heart and soul? Or has our mind already said, "This is what I will do. This is what I am going to do. Yes, I can see it done now, I can see it in my mind. I'm so great. I'll pray later or we won't pray at all, or who needs God? Look what I have done and now will do even more"? So now look at what you have done spiritually. You have just shut the door to the soul, God's connecting source. Your mind wants to make sure that no connection with God's spiritual voice or His knowing in your presence can be powerful enough to override the mind's decision. If the evil spirit does not have control of your mind, then why does your brain, your mind, continually make us suffer with wrong decisions that felt so good when we made them?

The king already has made up His mind to go to war, but to follow protocol, he should act like a righteous religious person, so he asks the man of God. His mind has made the decision, the door to his soul is shut, and now his mind wants to conjure up a confirmation to its decision by asking someone else's opinion. How many times we have done this and how many times have succeeded for a period of time but only to fail in the end result, time after time after time. Sometimes we don't even succeed, we fail, slightly or miserable sometimes finding great success but no peace or satisfaction in our efforts of accomplishment after all the work is done.

So the king hears the answer from Micah who has repeated the answer given by the false prophets, the worldly people without spiritual knowledge of God's plan for the kings life, Micah was being facetious. But the king in verse 16 says, "Don't be unkind, tell me in truth what does the Lord have for my life, speak the truth in the Lord's name." And Micah now speaks the truth in verse 17 and proclaims disaster for the king. Now in verse 20 the Lord speaks and asked the hosts in heaven, "Who will entice King Ahab to go into battle? Who will entice him to fail?" Verse 21 and a deceiving spirit steps forward and stood before the Lord, "I will be a deceiving spirit in the mouth of all of His prophets," the spirit says to the Lord. And the Lord commands the lying spirit to go and enter into the prophets, over four hundred men, and because the king believes what he wants to believe, the spiritual lie told to him brings about his death.

In the Old Testament, the Book of Micah chapter 4 verse 5 states, "Though all the peoples walk each in the name of his own god, as for us we will walk in the name of the Lord our God forever and ever."

Because we can walk after any spirit, chase him, catch him, be consumed by him, this is our own free willingness to believe whatever we want. Deep inside ourselves we believe what we decide, no matter what is told or commanded to us by other people: father, mother, friend, pastor, priest, fellow worker, the government, laws of any kind, police, teachers, politicians, on and on and on.

You and I make our choice, period. What lying spirit consumed me when I was an alcoholic? How many unclean spirits lived in me and continually told me how great I was, that if I tried hard enough I could accomplish anything I wanted to do. Money, lust, carnality, addiction, anger, frustration, hate, deceiving, lying, and so it goes, denying all the time that my failures were *my fault*. No, someone else always caused me to fail. To deny the truth is a simple way out for our mind to justify our being right, for others to be wrong. But to deny the truth about your life may be simple for your mind, but it is absolute, total destruction for your soul, and your walk will continually be out of God's will.

In repetition, again we ask who in you controls your actions, your daily life, monthly life, yearly life. Is your mind in complete control? If it is, then your fleshly body has and is making all the decisions for your life. The consummation, the consuming power to make fatal mistakes in our life is because the spirit and soul have not been acknowledged, not asked, not even thought of. Is your body and mind in control or is your spirit and soul in control? This is your choice! No one else is involved in this choice. In the world of the spirits, they watch and wait. Do you choose to let your fleshly body control your thoughts and consume your mind? Why is it we make this choice first? Because, it's easy, easier. A lying spirit enters into us, and as the king chose, so we choose. "My flesh loves to sin." We were born into it, why shouldn't we receive it as natural and enjoy it? Whoever told me my spirit, the true person of who I am, should be in control, that my soulish self belongs to the worldly spirits or the heavenly spirit. "Make a choice." One or the other is going to control my life and my decisions forever and ever. "How blessed is the man to whom the Lord does not impute iniquity and in whose spirit there is no guile" (Ps. 32:2). What is iniquity? Blessed is the person that does not have it. Who is it? Where did it come from? How did I get it? We go to the *Revell Bible Dictionary* for an explanation of the word *iniquity*:

1. The Hebrew word (*awon*) a willful twisting of or deviation from the divine standard. This means a willful twisting of God's divine spiritual laws and happily deviating from them.
2. The Greek word (*adduce*) suggests conscious human acts that cause harm to others in violation of the divine idea (page 516). So we are conscious of our sinfulness.

So we know now, openly and in truth, the unwillingness to follow God's divine words is very much the acts of our human nature, and such acts of disobedience will be justified by our mind. But now what about our soulish spirit? In the second part of that verse it plainly states, "and in whose spirit there is no guile." The American Standard Bible reads "guile" instead of "deceit." Deceit is falsehood, deception, a deceiver; are you and I deceivers by hiding our true self from our families, friends, neighbors, and most of all, ourselves? Am I deceiving myself when I say I can do this or I can do that, knowing full well I'm unable to accomplish the very thing I brag about doing or have done by failing miserably? Hollywood stars live in a world of acting; do they deceive the world in who they really are? Or should we believe their actions are who they really are? We may not be on the big screen, but are you and I putting on the act for our loved ones and family? Is it us or our job, to act out this way every day, because we are afraid to be ourselves and afraid of the hurt and unforgiveness of others, our inability to humble ourselves in front of them and be the changed person, living in truth not acting out deceitfulness every day in our life.

They will see this changed person, but many may say wait and see what he does or what she will do as time goes by. So if you decide to be changed spiritually and now your physical life changes, then you and I must know it's going to take time, like maybe the rest of our life. It's not going to be the instant greatest high you are looking for, as an addict looks for. It's not the reason; high is not the reason. Being an alcoholic, just one more drink so I can feel the freedom I need; it's a high no matter how you or I describe it. So some call it an "escape." Now that's humiliating, isn't it; escape from what? Just because I need to smoke a joint every day doesn't mean I want to escape from my problems, does it? I just want to be relaxed. I've been uptight all day. One joint doesn't hurt anybody. Well now, just because I like to drink a beer in the morning doesn't mean I'm a drunk.

Just because I like my whiskey and water doesn't mean I'm trying to escape. Escape what? I'm just trying to relax. So I drink a six-pack a day! And it goes on and on, snorting, shooting, smoking this or that, just actually doing what I want to do for a few minutes of my life, leave me alone. Some brag about their highs, others deny it.

But remember one thing: it's been going on around the world for thousands of years; this is not something new. It's as old as the time when Adam left the garden. That's when it began, make no mistake about it. Whatever in your life you use to get high on or escape from or relax with—booze, drugs, sex, authority over others, pride, vanity, eating, anger—if you enjoy hurting other people, it all makes you feel good, doesn't it? These are all spiritual lies, told to you and me as an excuse to prohibit us from reaching the real goal, which is letting me be me, letting you be who you really are.

These things in our life are not highs but lows. Escape is to be caught in the net by the trapper; relaxing in mind disorientation is putting oneself into a straitjacket. Bound up by a habit! Tied tight in a knot! Again and again the Bible calls it "chains." It has been said, "But don't call me a sinner, I'm not a sinner, I'm just trying to get through this life with some kind of enjoyment." But spiritually, you bind yourself tighter and tighter. Better you should listen to your soul, because the strong man cometh to check his traps, to check his net, and he knows our sin nature is weakening our ability to say "no" to the demon temptation. You and I have heard the old saying from the '60s, the hippie generation. "If it feels good, do it!" So as we end this conversation, be determined, start to think each day—why did you do these particular actions? Did you hurt someone today? How did it make you feel when you just started speaking before you started thinking about what actually should or shouldn't be said? Did you have your quiet time today? Were you at peace for at least one hour out of your busy day? Did you thank the Holy One for those unexpected but uplifting moments in your life today? Or externally did you do what you had to do today, but internally there was a void, a complete emptiness in what you accomplished this very day? Time after time, one abandons the presence of the Lord in our soul and spirit, and then there is nothing, like an empty house. And we stand alone in our thoughts, asking, "For what reason do I feel this way?" Could it be that you have become sterile in your spiritual life? Do you have a spiritual life? In our previous writings, we said repetition is good; it helps us remember especially spiritual things. The world offers nothing, remembers nothing. There is absolutely not one formula available in our life: for our life to change the outer person, by giving the inner person authority over the outer person, we now perceive the real you. There are many great minds today, greater by far than mine. Far superior are they than I in the knowledge and knowing of great and small subjects. I would be but filthy rags before these thinkers and proclaimers.

But since many things have been tried in your life and most have failed, let's take a deeper look into the spiritual world, the world they, the spirits, live in and work in twenty-four hours a day, seven days a week, month after month, year after year, century after century. Since time began, the spirit that changed Adam is the same spirit today roaming the Earth. The unclean spirits come in and go out of our world as Satan directs them. Each is trying to accomplish his or its orders and to cause us to struggle through each day.

By following our fallen nature, we are held captive in this routine for a lifetime, and we actually follow their agenda that they set. Is it now time to call yourself into spiritual action? To actually take control of this fallen sinful nature by believing that we can enter into the supernatural and deliver our self from the bondage of our sinful life? How can this be accomplished? How can I deliver myself from my own destruction? Because we are made in the image of God, body, soul, and spirit, we must make a choice. Deny there is a God in your life, or believe there is or will be God in your life. If God does not exist, your life stays the same; it will not and cannot change. Remember the absoluteness. Snow doesn't burn, well, this holds true here at this time. Now ask God to exist in your life, you have by your own free will decided to denounce your present way of life and now receive Him as your guide and companion. This is not some earth-shaking decision. One is forcing you, hammering on you, screaming at you, "You are going to fry in hell if you aren't born again." On and on and on! This is your decision. You decide if you want to walk into a new and different life. If you want to know the supernatural and the ways of your creator. Be still and reflect on who you really are, and in those quiet moments, make your choice. Are you a created being with a beautiful spirit and warm soul and can stand displayed with confidence to face today's struggle; or are you just born, plodding, plowing, and reaping of what the world says you can have and some get more and many get less? Maybe it's your luck. Are you lucky or unlucky? Did you know that luck cannot be found anywhere in your Bible? This God-inspired book, Old and New Testament, not one place or time does it mention "luck" or "lucky" or "unlucky," so since it's not Scripture, it puts it in the questionable category, who is calling for this or that to happen in our life? It certainly is not absolute. Luck is an unreachable situation, a word that describes nothing but can be applied to everything. Tears are shed. Unlucky is to blame again and again. Laughter and song, luck gets the credit for the good things, so let's enjoy our good luck! Luck did *not* make it happen. It's a meaningless word that the world uses to describe its accomplishments and failures that are brought on by spiritual beings warring after the person's soul. It's serious business whatever happens, happens for a purpose. The man who swept his house clean thought he was "lucky," but seven more came, and his "luck" changed, didn't it?

Your Creator who created you and I has created all things, and no one has ever lived on this earth without His consent. Read 1 Corinthians chapter 2 verses 14–16, "But a natural man does not accept the things of the spirit of God, for they are foolishness to him and he cannot understand them because they are spiritually appraised." These writings about spirituality make the people called unbelievers mad, anger arises in them, an emptiness is felt, "How dare you say I don't understand," "don't push your religion on me," "My mental capacity is far superior to yours," on and on. I didn't write it in its original form, Paul wrote it. And the world with its full of unbelief says, "We don't live by the old world because our society is far advanced," and we don't believe in spirits anyway. It's all foolishness. Look at your Bible, the Book of Isaiah 29th chapter, 14th verse. God is speaking through Isaiah and says, "I will take away the wisdom from the wise, it will perish from them, and understanding will be taken away from prudent men [clever men]."

So denying God is part of our sin nature, our natural self, the hard covering over our soul and spirit. The sin nature does not want the natural man or woman or child to have any connection spiritually with God, its creator. But the Lord has power over this sin nature, this hard shell that covers our spirit and keeps it captive in the dark recesses of our self, our house within each of us, where the true, real me lives. But God respects your own free will. He will voluntarily wait for you to make the call.

The decision to hook up, break the shell, and free the spirit and now with His help, you can make the change. Referring back to these two Scriptures, you can see that God's spirit has control over the minds of men if He so chooses. At any time or all times. It's really simple, if Satan lives in your house, then he controls your mind. If God lives in your house, he will give you your mind and his spirit;

now you have spiritual wisdom, now you have life. "Before you were dead, now you have life."

There is, as we all know, a great difference in day and night. These are absolutes in our life. We were not made to be nocturnal. We function best in the daytime, in the light. This is no great proclamation, no great verbalization, but is simply an understanding. When the Lord takes away spiritual wisdom from the wise men, they are left with nothing now but worldly knowledge. This now puts them in the dark spiritually. You and I cannot see our hand in front of our eyes in the dark of a natural setting. Pitch dark, totally blind, we are at the mercy of the thoughts in our mind that should, we assume, achieve our objectives, even though we walk in the dark. Some people around us that we depend on to walk in a spiritual darkness and are captive to the spirits of that darkness, and we depend on their decision for our place in life.

Now visualize what just happened. These people have their senses; they function very well and try continually to baffle us with their brilliance. But inside of each one is an empty space. They function in the dark. If you take something out of a space, then that space is void until something is put into the space. Now it becomes occupied. So if God takes away all spiritual wisdom and that means His God's wisdom, the space now is empty. The Holy Spirit, God's spirit, has left. It is now certain that the space will be filled.

Now how is it that empty places in our inner house are available? And to whom are they available to? So we go to our Bible and refer to Christ's explanation. Turn to the Book of Matthew (New Testament) chapter 12 verse 43: "Now when an unclean spirit goes out of a man, it passes through water less places, seeking rest, and does not find it." So a spirit, an unclean spirit with no name, was in this man. The spirit left for what reason makes no difference at this time. It passed through waterless places, out into the air traveling from place to place. It was looking for a resting place. Seeking rest and does not find it. This spirit wants to find for itself a warm secure place inside whoever, wherever. Verse 44 then says, "I will return to my house from which I came": and when it comes, finds it unoccupied, swept and put in order. So since the unclean spirit left, the man has done some serious thinking. Now he has put his life in order and for sure he must feel good about his new life. Because if the unclean spirit returned to find it in order, it must have been in disorder when he left it. Verse 45 says, "Then it goes, and takes along with it seven other spirits more wicked than itself, and they go in and live there; and the last state of that man becomes worse than the first, that is the way it will be also with this evil generation."

"Then it goes," meaning now, it, the unclean spirit, is coming back into the man. The unclean one went out and got seven more of his buddies to help him and they all moved into this man's inner house. Because this unclean spirit lost his place in the man's house, more than likely it was a weak familiar spirit. A habit that the man had for a long time. So the man says I'm going to break this habit and no longer obeyed the voice or urging to perform this particular function in his life.

Could it be that unclean habits are brought to us by unclean spirits who have been with us so long that we just assume its normal in our life?

He brought his buddies because they being more evil means they are stronger and more resistant to change. More powerful in their ability to control the man's nature. They protect the original unclean spirit from being evicted again. If the man didn't like his bad habit before, now he really is in trouble. We all remember times in our life when we tried to break a habit, "a new year's resolution," or "I'm going to quit this or that," only to find ourselves doing more of it the second time, and we succumb to the urging and fall back into our old habits.

So the man in verse 45 now has a life worse than his life with one unclean spirit, because now he has eight living in him; it certainly proves they are in control of his life. They made it worse didn't they? So does it seem feasible that if an evil spirit can make our life worse, then it must be a divine or Holy Spirit that can make it better? There has to be some correlation here. Why is something so simple so hard to understand. Remember the previous Old Testament verse of God sending a lying spirit to enter into the false prophets of the king. That lying spirit brought about the king's death.

Is my death or your death to be brought about by a lying spirit? We believed it, or believe something, for so long we knew it was the truth. It just has to be, I've always believed that way.

In my past I lied about things for so long they became part of my life. I couldn't remember if it was real or false. But I'm not alone, am I? God Almighty, God the Father, God the Creator of all things, the ancient God, He is above all spirits. He is the Almighty Divine Spirit. He knows all the spirits, who they are, why they are, where they are, how they are, and who is in charge of them at all times. The Scripture says all knees bow before God. Not only mankind but every spirit clean or unclean, angelic or demon, evil or righteous, all bend and bow down before Him and obey His every command.

In those lost years of my life, I, like many others, chased after money, career, family, the house, the car, truck, business, temptation, pride, arrogance, lust, stature, alcohol, and like some, fell like a stone into the total depths of a life and death struggle with addiction. A demon at that time I knew not. But years later met when I realized it was controlling my life.

Chapter 5
Why Christ and the Holy Spirit

Jesus Christ, the Son of God, leaves the heavens and His place beside God His Father and comes to earth as a human. Some believe it, some don't. As we have stated before in this writing, it makes no difference if they believe it or not. It's what I believe. It's what you believe. It's my choice. It's your choice. Their unbelief is their problem. That is their choice. I believe in spiritual absolutes. Christ now comes as a human person, yet not sinful. He has kept His divine nature, His spiritual nature, which is sinless. He walks and talks as a man but sees everything spiritual going on around him. The good, the bad, the ugly, He, Christ, sees it all because He can see both natures, spiritual and human.

So in His New Testament writings, He gives us the spiritual applications, how to apply our life spiritually to avoid the evilness ready to consume us in our worldly life. And today He is hated as bad as when He was hated then. Nothing has changed. Look around you, watch and listen, unbelief is in every corner of our world. They the unbelievers have their own gods. They themselves believe they are their very own god or some other person is god or whoever whatever. Who cares. There is only one God, Jesus Christ, the Holy Spirit, and God the Father. Christ said, "Before you try to take the splinter out of your brother's eye remove the log from your own" (Matt. 7:3). Mine was a log jam. I don't know about yours, but mine has logs backed up for miles. If they don't want to believe in the spiritual, I understand. I was there at one time in my life too.

So in their great hatred for Christ, they hung Him from the cross. The whole world knows this today. Whether they believe it or not is another thing. It's their choice. Now Christ leaves the earth and His replacement is the Holy Spirit. The very Spirit of God Himself. At no time in the history of the world does the Holy Spirit become more and more a movement among men, women, and children: This follows the very warnings of God through his prophets, who spoke in truth and were hated for it. Christ said, "I will send you the Helper" (John 16:7). The Holy Spirit is today yours and mine, for the time has come that he shall fall on all mankind. And do not be deceived, when you make the choice to receive him, the Holy Spirit, you will be hated by the world also. He, the Holy Spirit, is not an "it." He is the Spirit being from the very throne of God. He is the most powerful, the most awesome, most sensitive, most loving, most generous, most forgiving, most quiet, and with His own still voice overpowers all demonics, all unclean spirits, all of the filthy little familiar spirits that we call habits. The Holy One is over Satan himself and can, at any time, break the chains of unclean passions that bind us to our destruction. Down the road we go, bound and led by our daily routines, never finding time to stop and listen to the quiet still voice of the Holy Spirit speaking to our spirit through our soul.

Take your Bible out from under your bed or out of your desk drawer, knock the dust from its cover, and open the book to Ezekiel in the Old Testament, chapter 13 verse 24. The Spirit then entered into me and made me stand on my feet, and He spoke with me and said to me, "Go shut yourself in your house." So the Holy Spirit enters into Ezekiel. How can this be? Remember this excuse.

"Well, it only happened then, it doesn't happen like that anymore." "God really didn't say that did He?" And the unbelievers, the reasoners, those that must have proof. You and I can be sure we have heard all of these excuses why not to believe our Scriptures. Why not? To believe the Holy Spirit when He comes to you and says, "Be still and know that I am God" (Ps. 46:10–11). Go lock yourself up in your house, be still, read your Bible, listen, shut your mind down, it all takes time, but you must discipline yourself and break away from your old life for sure it will fight with you. The demons and unclean spirits that controlled my life for fifty years fought hard to hold on to their place at the table in my inner house. Years ago a good friend of mine told me as he was leaving our friendship, "My wife told me not be acquainted with you anymore, because you are filled with demons and have a demonic nature."

At first I just laughed. I wasn't at all familiar with that kind of talk. "It's a joke. Who does she think she is?" But I had to admit she was a very nice person. In later years I could see why she said what she said. But it was only after I had given myself to Christ that I was able to understand.

For those of us who talk nonsense, "all about me," all about everything and knowing actually nothing, listen to what the Holy Spirit can do for our life. Ezekiel Chapter 3 verse 26 says, "Moreover I will make your tongue stick to the roof of your mouth so that you will be dumb, and cannot be a man that rebukes them for they are a rebellious house." The Holy Spirit will have control of your mouth.

He can let you speak according to your righteous nature. When you are out with old friends that still enjoy their sin nature, then you may not have much to say. Surely you will not be talking godly things with them or to them because you will be dumb on that subject at that time. God says they are a rebellious house. Meaning their inner house is full of rebellion. Who causes rebelling against God? It wouldn't be the spirits of darkness in their house would it? Someday, when and if it comes, you will have to ask Him, the Holy One, to come into your life, help you make decisions, help you with your knowledge and understanding; your job, people in your job surroundings, school work and all things in your everyday life. Young or old, He, the Holy One, will open up your mind and let you see actually what is taking place in your life, who you are, really are. You will find peace forever and ever in your life because you will have an understanding that can never be known among men in the world that do not believe in the Spirit.

It is written that "thou shalt seek wisdom among evil men and shalt not find it." Old Testament, Proverbs chapter 14 verse 6, if you try to find this kind of wisdom in the world of your old buddies or the local pub crowd downtown at your old hangout, forget it. She is not there, she, Wisdom, does not hang out! The Holy Spirit sends Wisdom as a gift, not a gimme. Wake up. It's spiritual. Satan will send you his demonic buddies even if you don't ask for them. The Holy One waits to be asked, "Please help me," and only if it comes from our soul, not from our head or our brain that we cannot trust.

The Holy Spirit will bring to you the ability to discern or see by knowing the truth. And you will see the falsehood in trying to conspire with other persons in magnifying our own abilities. You and I must be able to see the Divine Son, our Lord, not just something that just might seem to be. There is a difference, this is the intent. We must be able to identify the absolute, the genuine, the truth, from the superficial imitations of today's life and lifestyle. It is only by our acquiring the Holy Spirit, who comes to live in us, that this can happen. As the Holy Spirit says, "It is done!" Now your new life begins. There is today an inclination toward the refusal of traditions in the churches of today's times. They speak of traditions being boring, the old way, like old people, musty, smelly, brain dead, out of touch with the times. We want music, loud and louder, noise and emotion, plenty of emotion. I'm not being critical, but we are being realistic. A pastor with his hair dyed red, spiked, earrings, blue jeans, and open shirt from his chin to his naval preaching on Sunday morning service about disciplining yourself; not by the old traditions of the church but by the new way, God's done a new thing. On and on.

I beg your pardon. What we want in our life, first of all, is stillness. Now we can be inspired by the Holy Spirit. His inspiration is genuine, His inspiration is absolute. His inspiring in you, our soul, in our spirit is beyond comprehension. Turn your Bible to the Book of Acts (New Testament) chapter 1 verse 5: "For John baptized with water, but you shall be baptized with the Holy Spirit many days from now." So as we are walking toward the door into the spirit world, opening ever so gently, we must have our ID in our inner house. First, our commitment to Christ, our receiving Him; second, our being filled with the Holy Spirit; third, our love of both Christ and the Holy One. As we have said before, this is not a gimme, it's a gift. Available to all mankind for those who believe. This is why the world cannot receive Him the Holy One. They choose not to believe, so they choose to be who they pretend to be, not who they really are. Remember again, it is written for you through Christ, "The world will not receive you when you receive Christ."

Acts chapter 1 verse 8, Christ is speaking, "But you shall receive power when the Holy Spirit has come upon you and you shall be my witness. Even to the remotest part of the Earth." Since my Lord Jesus Christ has spoken these words "you shall receive power," you can now count on, be sure of, it is the truth, it is genuine, this is an absolute. You will receive a new power in your life. Something you have never known or could know as long as you stayed in the world. This power is a spiritual power, an ability to go beyond your natural state. Now you have the power to make your habits change; now you have the strength to go forward in your life. Because now no evil spirit from the pit can hold you back. Even every demon, his knee shall bow before Christ. Those who live in you shall leave. Your spirit now comes out of its prison; it frees itself from the flesh. Your spirit demands authority over the flesh, demands the soul to reconnect to the Holy Spirit, disconnect its darkened self from the flesh. Old habits and beliefs will be discarded; new choices are made toward righteousness and truth. Now the inner war begins. Now a new foundation is being laid, cornerstone being Christ. A new foundation first, then a new temple for the Holy Spirit and all those that He brings with Him.

Acts chapter 2, verse 17, states, "And it shall be in the last days, God says, that I will pour forth my spirit on all mankind." In Acts chapter 2, verse 18 God also repeats again, "I will in those days pour forth my spirit." We can by choice choose His Spirit or choose the worldly spirits. Again and again it comes down to choice, your own free will. Christ says in making this choice you choose life or you choose death. It's your choice. Can't get much plainer than that. Life is with the Lord Jesus Christ, His Father the Creator, God of the ancients and all mankind and with the Holy Spirit. God calls Him "my spirit." Death is with the world, unbelief, disbelief, the idolatry, and all those who will not admit or commit to a life outside their own. The Holy Spirit knows the foreknowledge of God's will for your life. He can help you stay on track, help you through the bad times, and when there are bad times, heap gifts upon you beyond your human knowledge. Remember the song "I Did It My Way"? Wrong!

Remember in the Lord's Prayer we say, "Thy will be done," it means we will do it His way, the way He wills for it to be done.

So in making the decisions for change, no matter how old or young you are (or how good, bad or ugly you are), the time comes to see where you are now, where you're going, and how to get there. As we have spent time in talking about our choice and what takes place in making that choice, then let's open the door to their world a little wider. Since God said, "I will protect you going in and coming out," I can feel comfortable in letting us see what takes place in our life as we live each day in the world before committing our soul to Christ; we live in fear, in the fear of that final break away from the world. When you get ready to break away, don't listen to the voice of fear. His voice is like a barking dog. To begin with the demon is a fallen angel, one who followed Satan in his desire to overthrow God.

The demon is the enemy of the truth. We must continue each day to make ourselves correct our life. It will be a concerted effort to come against the beast whose main purpose is to snatch our soul and cast it down into the abyss of Hades.

Chapter 6
The Demon "Avarice"

Let us start with avarice. St. John Climacus calls him a thousand-headed demon. Now the demon Avarice is the lover of money, the worshipper of idols. He is the one who brings the fear and foreboding of old age. In the world, the lover of money sneers at the Gospel. Have you known a person that has said, "I made this money and I'll spend it the way I want to. I love material things!" We must conquer this passion for money and material things, because this feeling is brought on by Avarice as he sits in our inner house. In time he will cause you to hate the poor, and I know you have watched the person clench his fist over a dollar bill, go without eating, sleep in open filthy places so as not to spend one nickel. He causes us to make a bad example of ourselves as we try to look just like someone in our family or someone just down the street who acts the same way. What is wrong with these people, we ask? Answer, do you have a problem giving money to the church, what about helping the poor, what about your passions for material possessions? Have you ever gone out and bought food for someone who is too ill to work? Think about the voice in your head that says, "No, that's mine. Let him get his own," on and on. How long has it been since you said "I love you" to someone?

You can rid yourself of this demon easily by identifying him and rebuking him. Give a dollar to the poor man, share your things with other people who have nothing or very little. By prayer and discipline you can remove him from this room in your inner house. Be obedient to your Scriptures, trying to follow the commandments. It was said, "The man who has tasted the things on high easily despise the things below. But he who has not tasted the things above finds his only joy in his possessions." In case you didn't understand, it means the person who has tasted spiritually the things of Christ and heavenly powers now finds worldly possessions a stranger, being detached from all feelings money and material things bring. But if the person knows not the things of God, then he finds joy in his possessions and they become high priority in his thinking and his life.

In the early church, the Holy Fathers said avarice took third place in the eight deadly sins. So as we watch TV and see the big cars, the big homes, the fine clothes, it's all well and good what the world has to offer. Maybe your job is great, making mega bucks, buying whatever you want, any time you want it, so why would you worry about such things as a little dumb demon called, what was his name? "Avarice." He makes you and me the worshipper of idols that's all. No biggie. He just made you hate your neighbor. Do your clothes look just right for the occasion? Does your car fit the person you think you are? Maybe your education makes you think you are a step above the others around you.

With your clothes, your house, your car, your crowd you associate with, everyone around you thinks how great you are, they all envy you so much. "It feels so great to be idolized by everyone that knows me and not only that but by anyone who looks at me knows I've got it all together." Have you ever heard that voice before? Have you ever had that feeling, well, it's a passion. "It's my nature." No, it's your passion to have bigger, better, and more of it than your neighbor. You are passionate about who you want them to think you are. It's a passion. You covet these things or thing. Your passion controls your life, and Avarice is the authority behind that passion.

Open your Bible, New Testament, to Ephesians chapter 5, verse 5, "For this you know with certainty, that no immoral or impure person or covetous man, who is an idolater, has an inheritance in the kingdom of Christ and God." The immoral man and uncleanliness are demonics we will talk about later. But coveting is our subject now. Why in the world would a person who has as much as or more than he wants or she wants be interested in this anyway? Because we are not talking about the person we pretend to be, but we are talking about the inner person, the real you, the real me. The demon has a goal in mind, to overpower, to overpower you with his feelings so as they become your feelings. Now the more you enjoy the feelings of his strength, the more he holds you in his will. Your attention span for other things gets put aside, and as time goes by—weeks, months, years and years—he becomes stronger and we become weaker. But by this time we are consumed with our desire for our passions. "That's his passion." Remember one thing: do not ever forget this very important profound knowledge. The demon can never and will never be satisfied.

He will continually want you to want more of his feelings and sometimes the feelings of his demonic friends, now you are driven by their feelings also. So remember, the more you want and get, the more he wants you to want and consumes with all of your attention to your feelings for that passion; never are you satisfied, because like a drug you want your higher passion today, more higher tomorrow, and if you fail, you plunge downward. God forbid!

So as we climb up the ladder of success, Avarice is present with his feeling causing tremors of joy in our body. Now here come his buddies Pride and Vanity. Now for sure the person has taken a very hard spiritual hit. Now our spirit is condemned to darkness with absolutely no power over the flesh. The flesh is almighty and sooner than later becomes godless, spiritually. This is why our inheritance of the future, our spiritual retirement package, the promise of God's kingdom is in jeopardy. It's a spiritual law; it has nothing to do with what I say or what you say or your friends say or what society says. If you follow the material road all your life without the Lord first, then you will receive the reward at the end, by the world you followed during your lifetime. You have followed the Passion of a spirit that you loved more than Christ; the demon is hiding in plain sight.

It's been that way since Adam fell, and only since Christ came can we redeem ourselves by our willingness to change. The demon Avarice also brings a feeling of foreboding (bad or harmful) about old age. He tells us to get all our stuff around us, don't let anyone get anything, our old age is creeping in on us, the younger ones are coming to strip us of all our hard work, on and on and on.

To break his hold on us we must identify him, start giving to the church, the poor, the hurt, the family in need, the disabled, the monasteries, the organizations and the fund relief for victims of catastrophes. In your prayers ask the Holy Spirit and the Lord for forgiveness and ask to be delivered from this unclean spirit and now be obedient to Christ our Lord and not to any material thing. It is all well and good to enjoy all of the great abundance God gives us, but praise Him our Lord for all things spiritual and material things and never again say to yourself, "I am the Great I am." Again I say to you, listen—be still, shut your mind's voice down, unplug the recording that plays continually in your brain. Basic psychology 101 calls for "introspection"; look inside yourself and above all be honest, with you, yourself, your soul, your spirit, your physical self. There are great doctors of higher learning, great thinkers with vast knowledge on subjects of all known mind and health studies. We go to the men of learning and ask, "How can I control this passion?" for this is the ruination of my life! The law sends a person to prison because his passion for rape, murder, petty thievery, drugs, and the list goes on and on is so strong he or she must be put away to protect those of us who live a life free from their radical thinking and acting. But not always free from our own passions. The man of great learning now prescribes a pill, or let's call it a chemical, for my understanding of such things are very limited. But one thing for sure, the mind programs and the chemicals are all about the outer shell, how to change him or her to have a better life. Trying to change the inner person with the chemical is now a losing battle. The demonic spirit sits there in your inner room and laughs at the intense frustration, the person and people trying to make the change. Something so simple as a diet. How simple can it get? Try to lose weight. Take this pill, do that, eat this, and on and on.

Do you know that the spirit of Gluttony is in the higher realms of Satan's greatest demons? In your diet program, have you ever prayed against gluttony? Have you ever said, "I rebuke you spirit of Gluttony"? He controls your appetite. You know the feeling, don't laugh, remember the last holiday, all the good food, you ate and ate until you were full, so full you were almost sick, and what did you do? You went back to the table and said I just can't resist this dish, I've just got to have some more.

Like we said before, you can never satisfy the feeling the demon spirit sends through you as he wipes his filthy finger across your brain. He thrills your nature by his sinful presence, and you thrill him by your obedience to do his will, no matter how unlawful it is. Because this is kept secret doesn't mean it doesn't exist. So after we finish with Avarice, the demon of idolatry, love of money, and the son of unbelief, let us see how to release yourself or myself from his feeling, this knowing, this constant passion to get more, acquire more, live for material possessions and unbelief so strong you cannot realize your own demise, which could be at hand. The trap has been set. But you love it so!

Let's look at unbelief for a moment. So this demon, Avarice, has many different sinful qualities about him, and he manipulates man with his presence. Saint John Climacus says, "He Avarice is a thousand-headed demon." One of his heads is unbelief. We have in the last chapters talked about what Christ said about spiritual blindness. The New Testament is full of Scripture to confirm again and again Christ's truth about this subject. But as far back as the Old Testament, you can read Deuteronomy the thirteenth chapter and realize the anger God has for men and women and even cities who chase after other gods and make idols out of materials they acquired. But they will not believe He is their creator. Now don't get bored, don't yawn and say later on, "No more." Look to your Bible, the Book of Isaiah chapter 44, verse 7 through 28. God talks about He Himself, the Creator of all things, and he says in verse 8, "Is there a God besides me? I know no other." And He goes on to say about all that He has created, all things man uses to make himself comfortable. And man thinks he is becoming more and more the maker of things that God Himself furnishes to mankind. And from these materials God has furnished, man afterward kneels down and prays to the material as an idol and said to the material thing, "Deliver me, thou art my God." So from the very materials God creates for man's comfort, man turns his back on God and worships the material that makes him comfortable, leaving God out of his life and is happy in his own stupidity. Unbelief is now there, waiting, and when someone mentions God, the first words spoken are, "Now let's leave God out of this, okay?" Don't bring "God" into this conversation!

It's like if we take a large pair of bolt cutters or wire pliers and snip the spiritual tie wire reaching from God to our soul. Because our eyes can only see the greatness of our everyday materials and we cannot see our far greater union with our creator that we let him go, leave him out of our life, and now worship what we say "we have made." Now because we have violated the spiritual law of leaving God out of our life to worship that which we have made (out of His created substance), we separate our self from God. Our love for material, wood, steel, fabrics, money, whatever has blinded us spiritually. Now comes unbelief, watch now! Isaiah 44 verse 18 states, "They do not know, nor do they understand, for he has smeared [or shut] their eyes, they cannot see; and their hearts so they cannot understand." Because we live a daily life without God, we miss all the spiritual blessings, the gifts to be bestowed on us, and miss the most important aspect, our ability to see and understand, the knowledge it takes to make our life more peaceful, have more wisdom, and to attend to our life's decisions and judgment calls. Delivered from evilness that causes total destruction in our life having common sense to discern truth from hypocrisy and fraud, reject sexual misconduct, lustfulness, and being insensitive to other people's troubles. He, the man, who chooses to worship himself or his created idol has just made himself blind. He has absolutely no understanding of spirituality, and because he is blind, he is angry when he hears this. Now he is blind and dumb to the spirit. He who by his own choice has made himself this way wants to call you and me "fools" because we believe in something he cannot see or understand.

The spirit of unbelief has entered into this man's inner house and makes the man even more dependent on the demon by his rejection of God. More dependent on himself, which in time for all men is nothing more than clay to the earth. When man goes to the grave in this state, I think the Old Testament says it more appropriately,

"Their names are not entered in the book of Life." Since unbelief is so strong, it will become a passion if the demon continues to be more and more successful.

Unbelievers fall into many categories and can walk the walk and talk the talk of today's society. Pointing to their great success over adversities, or like many not so successful, they point to bad luck or worse yet, but more frequently blame their failures on someone else. "If it wasn't for this person or that person I could have made it." Have you ever used that one before? So the spirit of unbelief says there is "no God" or "God is gone somewhere else. I don't need Him anyway." And the person feels the rejection from what they think is God's presence and now the feeling of loneliness, a coldness sets into the soul of this person. The feeling of rejection from God or family or friends is what the demon gives us as he wipes his filthy finger across our brain. The very being that created you waits for you to make your choice—it's our choice—choose him or choose rejection; it's very simple. Most of the time we reject other people first, then they reject us because we blame them for rejecting us flat and on and on. "It's not my fault, it's your fault. No, it's your fault you did it first." We have all been through it, haven't we.

But what we didn't see was who was behind the problem. He's happy, he's thrilled, and now as things change in his favor, the unclean spirit enters deeper into our inner house and sets up bigger living quarter. Not for only himself but also his friends Avarice and Unbelief have a home. For him and his cronies, filthy friends. We have many books in our society telling us how to live; how to succeed; how to do whatever, wherever, whenever. So we hear as we grow up these are the laws of society. But how can I find a book, out of thousands of books, that will make a spiritual change in my life if society's ways are not working.

I want you to visualize all of the great books, the lesser books, all the books written that float in our society that do not pertain to God in any way. Stack them up, stack after stack after stack, mile after mile after mile. Society's answer to its wants and needs. No one can find time or place to read and consume all that has been written on how to adjust to society. What is society? Whatever society is. *Webster's New World College Dictionary* describes it as a "group of persons regarding themselves or itself as a dominant class usually because of wealth, birth, education etc." But it also says "it is a group of animals or plants living together in a single environment." So from out of this group, I should be able to find standards, ethics, and principles to live by. Does truth live here?

And now as you visualize the miles and miles of books, one appears alone and separate. Writing from thousands of years ago complied into one book, your Bible alone stands untouchable in time and place; not comparable to anything written spiritually in the history of the world. And we have a demon spirit that is so fearful of its divine spiritual writings that all he can say is, "It's not true." "Don't believe it, it's a waste of time, you can't understand it anyway." Too many thees and thous.

Society has thousands of books to explain why it is like it is and why we should follow their way.

God has one book and states in His book if you want the truth, "then test the spirit." Test this book, this one book against thousands of books that tried to help change our life, having a better understanding. The testing for thousands of books fails miserably. You cannot change your life or you cannot see why you are like you are if you listen to society. A man from Georgia said of some of the great minds, the intellectuals, the professors and politicians that influence our thinking and run our government, "Many of these people do not have enough common sense to 'park a bike straight.'" Our definition of worldly knowledge will explain why this is so true.

Common, a word describing the public or people in general, something all or many may know, such as common knowledge/basic, simple, having no rank, as a common person or common soldier. *Webster's Dictionary* says "not of the upper class" but to the public in general. Sense, a word Webster's describes as "the ability to think or reason soundly, normal intelligence and judgment, often as reflected in behavior." So if we take the word *common*, something that the general public knows and is basic reality to most people, and add *sense* to it as "reflected in behavior," then we are describing people who have common knowledge and behave rationally or behavior that is accepted by the public in general. Then it should be common sense to see and obey the laws of our country, our cities, our communities, and within our family. We acknowledge the presence of the divine spirit in our life if we so choose.

So we start with the family. Common sense tells us one man, one woman in marriage. I will not get into the other opinions on marriage. Now children become involved and soon we have a family. Not too hard to see and understand. Principles, standards, and ethics are now the forming nucleus for the family or group. If the right standards and ethics are taught and the right principles are applied, then common sense tells us this family should live happily ever after. So the father and mother who may be unbelievers read all the best books and receive the best advice and raise their children accordingly will find somewhere in the process that one child or more will not perform according to those teachings—in other words, a problem child, maybe an embarrassment to the family. I am sure we all understand, knowing some children and adults that have gone astray. Myself included! So in the same neighborhood, a father and mother who are believers in today's religions or have a belief in Christianity raise their children accordingly to the best books and teachings found, and they add their Christian lifestyle and beliefs into the growing-up process of the children. Now only to find that they also have a problem child or children. So as we grow up, we find our own likes and dislikes; we find ourselves looking at our life before us and look at our past we left behind. Some good, some bad, some ugly.

Chapter 7
Common Sense

What happened to common sense? In all the turmoil of life and family, common sense left. He said he wasn't needed or said he wasn't used or said he just got tired of waiting. The early saints of the church called the words "simple." Common sense to them was "simple." Not something today's man or woman or child wants to be described by. We all are hard drivers, running a fast tractor over unplowed ground, climbing the ladder of success, dealing and betting on our decisions each day.

Simple people, simple-minded—we are not simple. But in the world of the demon spirit, they of the darkness, simplicity is their great strength, for they have been using the same procedures for thousands of years. And the laws they operate by are absolutes. They cannot change or defy or in any way violate the spiritual laws that have been put in place for them and their kind. So they attack and retreat upon command, always staying in the same channel or on the same track, never able to disperse their individual power into an overall blanket effect. But they may attack and retreat in numbers, each one using its power with its companions, with another spirit or many spirits to cause a blanket effect. In their attack they bring their own power, only their own power, some weaker, some stronger, but each with its own individual feelings. The spirit demon, Fear, cannot cause the feeling of confusion. Feeling of the unknown is caused by the demon Fear. Being confused and disoriented can be caused by a demon, and it only. But the two together cause confusion and fear, feeling confused and the feeling of fear when we become disoriented or lost. I am sure I will get a lot of flack on this subject. The first thing I'll hear is "You can't prove it." But you can prove it by your own experience in life. Think of the times you became afraid and didn't know how to react to that fear. Some run, some, stand motionless unable to move, some say "I don't know what to do." Some will say these are just human reactions and have nothing to do with spirit or demons. Have you ever been around a person or have known a person that is afraid to leave their home, afraid to go to the store alone, afraid someone is going to harm them, afraid someone is following them caught in the net of the trapper they stay lost until someone gives them a pill to stop their anxiety? But the chemical wears off and the person feels powerless and is unable to cope with life's events, if that's not fear and confusion try putting on their shoes. Loneliness enters into this group when the others are ready. No one loves me. I'm all alone. Why can't I find someone, why? What do I do wrong?

No one cares.

Saint John Climacus step 24 states, "Simplicity is a constant habit of the soul that has become immune to crafty thinking." So to deliver ourselves from the attack we encounter each day we spend in their world, let us attract ourselves to the Lord. Draw near to Him, as disciples draw near to the master, simply, without hypocrisy, without double dealing, without cunning, without deception, without slyness and being crafty or using craftiness as we have done in dealing with others. The Lord wants the soul that comes to Him to be simple, free from all the abovementioned, free to become humble before Christ. And as you stand before Him in your simple nature He will receive you and now love you and cleanse you of all of the above deceptions. Do not put anyone on a pedestal, wife, husband, child, lover, friend, anyone. Do not give them your God love. That love is for him and Him only.

If you give them your God love, they will crush it; they will control you with it. Give God His love; give them your natural love. This is where many people get hurt in life. They give the soul's love for God to a person, and that person is not able to comprehend this deep love from the soul. So they, over a period of time, destroy that deep love. The shallow, natural love they offer does not last I am the pile of filthy rags as I come before Christ, full of sin and perversion. But I am like the animal that does not answer back as his master yokes him, but follow wherever he is led. An upright soul will do this for his master, in complete simplicity I come before Christ each day.

Forever and ever.

Christ Himself spoke of this in the Book of Matthew 19th chapter 23rd verse. Look it up in your Bible, don't take my word for it, and read it yourself. Verse 23 says, "Truly I say to you it is hard for a rich man to enter the kingdom of heaven." Why the rich man? Why single out the rich person?

The first thing that comes to mind is money, lots of it. Remember Avarice, the thousand-headed demon, the demon who brings us the feeling for "love of money"; the more you get, the more you want. He also creates the feeling of unbelief. God really didn't do that, did He? God didn't say that, did He? God didn't mean that, did He? On and on and on. "God doesn't have time for you and me. He's over in Europe or South America." He doesn't have time for us peons. They never stop in their unbelief. Remember, Avarice brings us the foreboding of old age. Foreboding means the prediction of something bad or harmful to come upon you. Remember when some of us passed forty, oh, a fear swept over us as we see old age coming soon upon us. Avarice and fear together does a number on us and we think it's normal. We just receive it and get anxious. All in life, right?

Wrong! No, we do not have to receive it and live with it. Remember Avarice is the feeling of idol worship. Have you ever asked yourself why man wants to worship everything else but God his creator? Everything that is available to mankind has been created by God for mankind, and we take His creation in our hand and look upon it, talk to it, love it, and our mind becomes full of it and our sin nature feeds on it. Makes us feel so good and it becomes an idol, something we just idolize.

Have you ever talked to your car? Sure. Have you ever talked to God in the same simplicity? So Avarice the demon sits inside God's created being and will not let go; he's there in secret. Nobody ever told me he was there. When have you heard the name Avarice mentioned on your TV Christian networks? Jesus Christ said as long as he sets in your house and you believe in what the demon tells you and you act out his orders through feelings he creates through your sin nature you are not welcome in the Lord's house, His kingdom. The place for you and I will stay vacant until we become a soul, simple and humble, before Christ, not proud of our material things, our money, or our idols. The Book of Luke chapter 23 verse 34 as Christ hangs from the cross, He said, "Father, forgive them for they know not what they do." And so it is with us as we are caught up in our daily life and all of the priorities we decide are important to us, for us, and many overriding factors brought upon us unknowingly, we turn our back on God. Christ asking God the Father, the creator of mankind, for you and I, to forgive us as we follow the mind-set, the feelings, the leading of our mind, following our sin nature, which unknown to us is from those who hate God, and bound hand and foot we joyfully follow the spirits of darkness, the very enemy of our Creator, embracing spiritual deformity as if it were truth. "Lord forgive us, we know not what we do."

This is why we must become open to stillness. Stop the rush! Stop and be still. In your stillness admit to yourself who you really are. Not pretension or cunning. So in your stillness you must become simple, a simpleness, void of all that is around you and surrounds you. I became meek and humble before Christ, before God the Father, the Holy Spirit. They are my only way out of the rebellion and terror that grips me. My rebellious mind does not want to conform, to submit to my simple soul, my quiet spirit to love the pure strength and truth Christ promises us. "Meekness is a rock overlooking the sea of anger, which breaks all the waves that dash against it, yet remains completely unmoved." On meekness, simplicity and complete lack of craftiness and cunning which comes not from our nature. But with a conscious effort, we can release ourselves from spiritual passions. Not only Avarice but all others that war against us. As long as our sin nature, our hard covering controls our thinking and actions, we will never be at peace. We will constantly be in turmoil and be unable to be in control of our life. Darkness will control our life because our sin nature is a servant to it and all or some of its fallen angelic occupiers. If you think you are in complete control of your life and all of that around you, you are living in spiritual delusion. God can command your soul to leave the earth, and at any time death will pull you off your throne. You may be experiencing the sweetness of your sin nature now at this present time, but this feeling of sweetness in your soul's realm is sugar spread over rat poison. If you spread rat poison on a piece of bread and cover it with sugar, you cannot taste the poison, but in the end result you will receive the suffering of the poison, not the joy of sweetness. When you and I live in this land of sinful sweetness, joyful and comfortable in our ability to control our destinies, without a spiritual covering from God, we are living in a land of fantasies. Surely the evil one smiles.

We have spent much time on simplicity and stillness. Why? Because this is the beginning of spiritual awareness. God's presence. The Holy Spirit will not ever enter into your inner house and rebuke the others living there unless we want to change. For Him, the Holy One, to come into you, we must be still, humble, meek and unafraid, and ask for a change in our life. It is said, he who loves stillness shuts his mouth; he who delights in talking and wanders about telling everyone how great he is will be driven out of his house by this and other passions. The man or woman that has become aware of their sins has controlled his or her tongue, but a talkative person has not yet come to know himself as they should. Your first clue should be "well, in my opinion." Does anyone really care?

Once you and I become a friend with stillness and silence, we can draw near to God, and by secretly conversing with Him, we can be enlightened by God. With stillness and simplicity we walk and wait, we become humble and meek before our Creator, and now out of this comes innocence. We must make that conscious effort to commit our self with innocence to innocence. This takes work, spiritual work, yet when accomplished, the virtue of peace will be given to those that prevail.

We as small children born into a world of deception and sinfulness are innocent of its surroundings. But as we grow older, we are more susceptible to following our own sin nature, some temptations more powerful than others. As we spoke before, families have problem children whether or not they come from good homes or bad homes, believers or unbelievers, makes no difference. They stumble and fall, and as age continues they find false pleasure in the darkness offered to them by the spirits of our world. They listen to the voice, "Go ahead. No one will know! Lie about it. It's easier than telling the truth."

The evil spirits, those that disobey God and His laws, they hate innocence. Innocence is a sign of cleansing or of being clean. They want us in bondage to them, heaping guilt upon us for who we are in our sinful nature. And after we taste the sweet taste of sin, they bring guilt, with the soul and spirit suffering under guilt's desire; he drives us deeper into despair. So it is with man and women that attack children. For example, men molesting little girls, they want the child's innocence; they want to destroy the child by taking away its innocence. So here they come with their cunning and deception, planning the rape, feeling the sensation of the moment when they can have the child alone. To take them in that moment of lust, extreme lust caused by the demon of lust who has taken his filthy finger and wiped it across the man's brain, came into him, and made his nest in the man's inner house. This causes such an explosion of passion and ecstasy. The man now is out of his natural control, but not out of demonic control. The demon wants that innocence. He feeds on the destruction of that innocence, knowing full well that the child after being raped and beaten into submission will never be able to know innocence or have a clean inner self. If they live through it. Lust and guilt will stay with them forever tormenting them and never will leave until this act is given to Christ totally. Now the healing begins. Christ commands the Holy Spirit to evict the unclean spirits out of the person and now the Holy One brings peace and rest, love and strength to that tormented soul.

Both the raped and the rapist must turn to Christ, if not the raped will be sick forever, never able to rid them self of the flash back and trauma it caused. And the rapist, he will go on in his demented nature attacking one child after another, thrilling each time he destroys the innocence of the child or person he is attacking. All the time the attacker is under the influence of Lust, being the powerful demonic that it is, cannot ever be evicted without Christ. Speaking

Christ's name means nothing to some people, but to the demon, the name of Jesus Christ brings an unbearable torment and he will leave. His knee will bend. Go before Christ, be still and be simple and humble, ask for forgiveness, and try to be obedient to God's nature and His ways. Not your own. And because you did not know who you were following and did not know whose influence you were under, He, Christ, will forgive you, and your innocence that was stolen from you long ago shall be returned to you, its rightful owner. Do not listen to fear as you get yourself prepared to make this choice. The unclean spirit of fear is the first to say, "No, don't go there; you're going to lose all of your freedoms to do what you want to do. For the rest of your life you will live in bondage to that God of laws and stern discipline. Stay as you are. Things will get better. Maybe your luck will change."

Now your soul may be in a deep and weakened position, from years of being a slave to the power of demon passions or to the feelings they generate by their presence in us. The soul wants to be free, and it sends its weak voice to the brain: "Go to Christ, set me free." But Fear says, "Hey, Guilt, I need help," and Guilt says to the person, "You're too sinful, no god wants you. Look at yourself, you're a wretched wreck." Now they cry out to Lust and Perversion. "Hey, we need help!" This demon says as he approaches the person, "Now if you go over to the side of Christ, you can no longer enjoy my feelings of passion in wanting sexual gratification, because the church will stifle your wants, and you need sex and perversion; it's not allowed in the church." And they keep calling more and more into your house, taking up the battle cry, forcing the weak voice of the soul to be drowned out, and the last and loudest voice of all is from a demonic Gluttony, the strongest and most powerful voice. Gluttony creates a feeling of hunger and says, "Let's go eat something and think about it; we'll make a choice later on." And the soul of that person loses round after round after round, because the mind listens to the voices of darkness, and emotion grips the body in its tight grip, consuming the feelings generated by the passion that each demon possess individually, that never-ending attack, lie after lie after lie. Lord have mercy on my soul.

"Things which eye has not seen and ear has not heard and which have not entered into the heart of man, all that God has prepared for those that love Him" (Isa. 64:4). So before we come to Christ, God said, "You cannot see or hear because first it must be put in your heart." Now, once Christ is put in your soul or heart, now you can see the lies of Satan and hear the voice of God, being now able to discern the truth from the lying spirits who have kept you away from all of the things that have been prepared for you in your life. These good things have been waiting in storage for you and your commitment to believe in Christ.

New Testament, 1 Corinthians, chapter 1, verse 9 declares, "God is faithful through whom you were called into fellowship with, His son Jesus Christ our Lord." Now when we believe, not if we believe, God's word is absolute truth and can be held in our soulish depth for a force that can turn death away and give us life forever. For a belief so strong that under any circumstance you can say, "I believe that God will deliver me from this and now I shall wait, even until my death." For His word is unyielding and non-negotiating. So with this belief in my soul and mind, bone and tissue, I can say when we believe in Christ our Lord, God the Father, the Creator will now fellowship with me and be faithful in His ever present power to drive away all darkness that tries to consume me. God's commitment to you is not negotiable, nor is your commitment to Him at any time negotiable. Some live in a world that no longer has any standard, ethics, or principles. We find ourselves left without guidance, without a knowledge of right or wrong. "Oh, yes! I know right from wrong." "I'm not stupid." Well, do you observe right from wrong, and do you apply it in your life? A person can act like Mr. Clean, but when temptation comes and calls his name the person looks both ways to make sure no one is watching and now smiles, and opening his soul, he consumes the temptation, and at a later date, when he has been found out, he quickly blames others. "I know you have never seen this person!" "Not you?" Did our Lord Jesus Christ say in the Lord's Prayer, "Lead us not into temptation but deliver us from evil"? Of course it's not the Demon Temptation, that fellow who comes to you and me and says, "Go ahead, no one will ever know." Do you ever think you're the only one who has felt the voice, because your friends will tell you, "You don't hear voices, do you?" Of course it's just natural. Temptation is a way of life. Don't look for a demon behind every bush! Don't believe those religious fanatics. On and on and on.

There was a pastor in my early life as a Christian. I had turned fifty-two and was seeking spiritual guidance because I knew truth is spiritual, not physical, and I wanted to confirm it, not wait for it to be confirmed. Sounds natural, doesn't it? In our spiritual discussions he told me, "Don't look behind every bush for a demon. Life has many natural habits and ways to live without looking over your shoulder for the bad guys. They are not always there." Two years later he lost his church, his whole world of hard work and sacrifice, and went down in the flames of anger and rebellion. His family, friends, and congregation fell into a state of judgment, each pointing his or her finger at the others.

So what happened yesterday or last month or last year, or one hundred years ago, or maybe as far back as Adam? It's the same demonic spirit today. He was there yesterday. He was there last month, last year, one hundred years ago, and was with Adam when he fell to Temptation and had to disconnect from God's presence. Same guy, same feeling generated as he wipes his filthy finger across our brain and expects us to grab a moment of his ecstasy that he shoots through our veins. But when we are caught, well, who comes to our rescue but Temptation's buddy, Denial? They work together, feed together, laugh together, follow Satan's commands together, but are two distinct separate beings. Temptation can only tempt us into doing something against God's word. Only God can deliver us from this evil. Denial comes to the rescue for Temptation and other lying spirits, every evil spirit. But caught by the exposure of truth, they become powerless.

Adam did not wish to say "I sinned" but said rather the contrary of this and placed the blame for his transgression upon God who created "everything good," saying to Him, "The woman whom thou gavest to be with me, she gave me of the tree and I ate." After Adam, Eve placed the blame on the serpent. And they did not wish at all to repent and be forgiven of Him. Are you in denial? It's the drugs' fault, it's the alcohols' fault, I can't control myself, it's not my fault. It's my circumstances, why is everyone against me, I'm helpless. Lord Jesus Christ, Son of God, have mercy on our souls.

St. Symeon the New Theologian (949–1022), in Homily #45, he writes back in the tenth century.

> Do not say that it is impossible to receive the Spirit of God. Do not say that it is possible to be made whole without Him. Do not say that one can possess Him without knowing it. Do not say God does not manifest Himself to man. Do not say that men cannot perceive the divine light or that it is impossible in this age. Never is it found to be impossible my friends. On the contrary it is entirely possible when one desires it. (Hymn 27; 125-132)

This is the knowing of a saint from the tenth century. For you who have a problem with saints and their writings, I ask you before you pass judgment on them (because of what other church leaders have said) read the saint and his writings. To you who confess the knowledge of saints immaterial in today's life struggle, I ask, "Why didn't we see them in the twentieth century? Where is your spiritual father? Hiding under a bushel basket where you cannot see his light?" We can see the physical Christ, but the unseen, the divine Christ, in the Spirit, we do not acknowledge. At the same time, we are thinking of Christ as some super human being, when He has made man. Putting man into an invisible spiritual body, sinless and non-corruptible. He now looks normal, because we cannot see the divine nature or spiritual body that He has come to earth with. He, Christ, was always in this divine nature or spiritual body and therefore, on earth He always had two natures: one human, one spiritual. This is why He, Christ, could see all things spiritual going on around Him, while He looked so human to all that knew Him. When He spoke to the demons, when He told people what they were thinking, their past and their future and saw who was inside of the person or persons around Him.

To partake or to participate in this ability to see the spirit world around you, you must be able to have a nature, a divine or spiritual nature. You and I are not born with this nature, and therefore we cannot see into their world, the world of the spirit. Therefore the unclean ones have an advantage over us. They can try to move us to do their work, their bidding, always looking inside of us to see who's there. The evil ones and also the heavenly ones, they all partake of you and me in our lifetime, depending on our willingness. Remember these writings are not for everyone. Much flak and verbalization will come against this thinking and these writings. But if you truly want to change who you are, without doctors or chemicals, without asking another human being, spend time contemplating and thinking about your withdrawal from the world, and ask Christ to deliver you from your sinful nature, to receive through Him your divine nature, with discipline and determination you do your part, He will do His part. This is a spiritual absolute.

You were created for a purpose. That purpose is not, surely was not, for you to spend a lifetime being pummeled by some dumb, aggravating, inconsequential unseen being, overpowered by it only because you could not see or understand its presence in your life. Remember our Lord Jesus Christ tried to explain to His people the spiritual significance of how actions in a person's life bring on positive or negative reactions to circumstances in our life at that time. So let us do the same. Look at this parable as in the flesh, but try to see how it's spiritually part of our way of life. When the master of the house asks a servant from the fields to come and enter into work within the walls of his household, he stipulates to the servant that he must stand in the rain naked before the master, washing the grime and soil from his or her body, and the water from heaven brings a cleansing to this servant that he has never known before. Not only does the flesh become cleansed but the soul also. The servant in his or her obedience to stand and be washed with the master's living waters finds the feeling of peace and love that was never known to them before, as they had all their life worked in the fields outside the walls of the master's household. And when they enter into his household, their clothes are presented to them, clean, pressed, and washed so that the colors that were faded are even brighter now. The servant now joins the others that have entered before him, taken in and joyfully accepts the work that must be done, obedient to the Master's call at any time.

But what about the servant that is called and will not stand naked in the rain to be washed by the master's living waters? He thinks by standing in the rain with his clothes on he is washed as were the others. Ashamed sometimes, defiant sometimes, the unclean servant denies the master's household principles and standards, as real and in truth, but uses them for his own deceiving nature to enter through the door of the master's house. Since he stood in the rain with his clothes on, his body is still soiled and grimy from his days in the field. The sweat from his years of labor still covers his nature. His soul remains in the prison of his flesh. But his clothes are washed clean from the rain and he enters the master's household, into labor with the other servants.

Does this person, the servant, really think he is disguised by wearing the right clothes and saying the right words, that the master who has watched the whole thing, the servant's disobedience, his shame, his ignoring the ethics, principles, and standards of the household rules are not worthy for this particular servant? Does he really think he has not been seen? This servant may wear the right clothes and say the right words, but the far greater and the most important things they have not received and will not ever receive are the virtues of peace, love, repentance, grace, and a pleasing relationship with the master, and the joyful experiences given to those who came naked and open, obedient to the master's call, obedient to his wishes, trying hard to work within the rules of the standards set, the ethics needed, and the principles applied to receive wisdom and knowledge. The unclean servants cannot understand, nor will they ever understand, unless they too stand naked and unafraid before the Master, letting the living waters from heaven wash away their worldly ways, their souls open to the spirit, and as time passes, the other servants see also this person's true self and may receive him or her as one of their own;

but for you who are working and trying to act out your duties as a servant of God, to receive a status symbol or receive the gifts from the Master, or for your own personal gain through pride and vanity, lying and deceiving and causing trouble for your Christian brothers, we know you. You are not clean before God. Your unclean spirits give you away. Your unclean spirits within you will never let you be like those that stood before God and asked to be cleaned, naked, and unashamed. They came to be washed, and so must each of us if we expect to receive the virtues that are given to those that are worthy.

Chapter 8
The Law of Life or Death

Now let us go back to the year about 69 AD. A man by the name of Ignatius was appointed the second bishop over the church of Antioch, in the city of Antioch in Syria where Paul and Barnabas came as missionaries. Paul the apostle was martyred sometime between AD 64 and 67 in Rome, and since he was a Roman, he could not be crucified, so he was beheaded. These were the formative years of the church. Because Ignatius was a striking person of faith and loved our Lord Jesus Christ and was a firm believer and leader in the church, he was arrested and brought to Rome to be torn apart by wild beasts. The ancient church historian Eusebius dates this happening somewhere in AD 98–117. In the book *The Apostolic Father*, the detail of St. Ignatius's travel to Rome under armed guard is not especially pronounced, but we do read about his letters written to the different churches as he passed through their areas on his way to be martyred.

In his letter to the church at Ephesus in Asia, as St. Ignatius was passing through under Roman guard, he writes, "Men of flesh cannot act spiritually, nor can spiritual men act fleshly or in a fleshly way. Faith cannot perform the deeds of unfaith. Nor can unfaith perform the deeds of faith. But what you do as believers in Christ in the flesh is spiritual because we do all things in Christ." St. Ignatius is teaching from Paul's writings in the Book of Romans, New Testament, chapter 8, verse 5 through 13. From these writings, we know that in our early church years the man of great writings, like St. Ignatius and others, the church was not spiritually dead in all of the years until our present time, as some men say it was. For those men that write the church was dead at any time since Christ are themselves spiritually dead. For they work in the flesh only. For if the church was dead spiritually at any time, then it would not have survived these many years. So it is as Paul writes in Romans chapter 8, verse 2, "For the law of the spirit of life in Christ Jesus has set you free from the law of sin and death." How is this? What does it mean to you and me as believers and nonbelievers? First, Paul states that there are two laws, the law of the Spirit of life and the law of sin and death.

Now to understand what depth lies here we must understand the total significance of each statement.

First, the law that he talks about is a spiritual law, or as we said earlier, an absolute. This is not a man-made law to be broken by some and obeyed by others. This is a commitment, given by God to man at his creation. God our creator promised this to us in the covenant of the Old Testament and the New Covenant with Christ. It's a spiritual contract between man and God. God does not break His promise as He waits for man to commit and spiritually sign or pledge himself to this contract or covenant. So when you accept the Master's call and come to be washed clean and your soul and body ready to enter the Master's house, this law, this statement in the contract says when by receiving Christ the Master we in return receive life, this new life is free from the laws of the past, sin, and death.

All of the time spent by thousands of men writing through thousands of years means nothing if we do not understand basic "one on one" why we must come to Christ. Why the spiritual contract with Christ is only good to those who pass through the door to His Kingdom. Coming with our soul naked, to be washed free from sin and death by their own willingness to receive God their Creator through Jesus Christ, our Lord and God. As you pass through Christ spiritually, you now enter into Him, and when that happens, you now receive the Spirit of life. The Holy Spirit entwines with your spirit and so begins your new life. That is why Christ said to Nicodemus in John chapter 3 verse 3, "Truly, truly, I say to you, unless one is born again, he cannot see the Kingdom of God." By making a spiritual commitment, we receive a spiritual life. In verse 6, it says, "That which is born of the flesh is flesh. That which is born of the Spirit is spirit." We are born in the flesh and will be fleshly and worldly until we commit to the Spirit of Christ, now we become spiritual and let ourselves fall into the arms of Christ. Amen. You have now received the spiritual power to awaken your soul, your understanding. You now can see spiritually all of these virtues to set you free from your past and its bondage. This prison door has just opened you can step out into the light; you can and will find peace inside yourself forever.

All of the electric tools lay in your shop waiting for you to electrify them so they can do your work for you, but until you electrify your spirit with Christ, all of these spiritual tools cannot be workable or usable; they lay waiting for you as do your tools in the shop. There is no religion, no belief, no other faith in this world that can cause a spiritual interaction with the Spirit of life, the Holy Spirit, nothing except through your union with Christ.

The second law is the law of sin and death. When you and I refuse Christ and His Kingdom, we accept sin and death as a way of life. All of the power, spiritual power, that is available through Christ lays dormant, futile, unusable, and unavailable. This spiritual law is as absolute as any other spiritual oath given by God from the beginning. To live under this law brings condemnation. Those who walk in the flesh think in the flesh, and will continually set their mind and live their life in their sin nature.

This is a principle, a principle set in stone. The Ten Commandments, ten principles for the original Hebrews to live by. Why? Because God's ways are spiritual, not physical. So for us to come out from under the principles of sin and death, we must receive into ourselves new principles, God's spiritual principles, which sometimes defy our physical logic and therefore are not consumed by our thinking in the flesh. It seems impossible for those that do not believe to conceive this transformation and what can happen in a person's lifetime if they commit themselves spiritually.

In those days of my addiction and those years of my determination to "do it my way," I had at times a blank happening, a feeling like my head is filled with concrete, a total unknowing in my head. I could not understand why. What is this blank that is a thought but a knowing or understanding of nothing? My whole self is consumed by this happening. Everything in myself at that moment is shut down. I want to release myself from it so that I can see what I should be seeing but to no avail. In these times a hopeless and incompetent feeling washes over me, and my inner struggle is told to no one, but I am left weak and dysfunctional inside myself. Since my conversion to Christ as my Lord and Master over my life, I have not at any time experienced this lost and incompetent feeling. Once we pass through Christ, all things shall be washed away.

Chapter 9
The Transfiguration

Open your Bible to the New Testament, the Book of Matthew chapter 17, verse 1 through 9:

> Now after six days Jesus took Peter, James and John his brother, led them up on a high mountain by themselves. And He was transfigured before them. His face shone like the sun, and his clothes became as white as the light. And behold Moses and Elijah appeared to them, talking to Him. (Matt. 17:1–3)

The transfiguration of our Lord Jesus Christ from the physical to the spiritual is to show how He the Christ is of two natures: one spiritual and one physical. His face shines like the sun; we ourselves cannot look directly at the sun because our eyes cannot stand its brightness. Therefore, the clothes that cover Him shine bright as light. Put a sheet over a bright bulb at night and the white sheet or cloth becomes whiter and brighter. And so as Christ's divine nature is a pure radiant white light shining so bright, now two men appear with him, Moses and Elijah, who are also in the Spirit and they appeared talking to Him. Peter, James, and John witness this moment, when Christ in His divine majesty is seen by men with the naked eye, to be able to tell the others what they had seen and heard, but not until the appointed time. Remember now, Christ had shown the men that followed Him, His disciples, His divine power many times—healing the sick, bringing sight back to the blind, hearing to the deaf, bringing back to normal, deformed limbs, and many other acts of divine power—but this is the first time for them to see His divine nature. This is the divine nature that you will receive when you and I come to Christ in total willingness and a repenting of our past life.

In your Bible, 1 Corinthians, chapter 2, verse 9, Christ made this promise: "But just as it is written, things which the eye has not seen and ear has not heard, and which have not entered the heart of man all that God has prepared for those that love Him." Where is it written? Christ spoke it, and He said, "Just as it is written," where we want to see it written. Turn your Bible to the Book of Isaiah, chapter 64, verse 4. Oh of Isaiah's greatest achievements have been when the Assyrians threatened to destroy Judah. Isaiah's pleading to God was heard by the Almighty and the entire army of Sennacheribs were destroyed. Read about the battle, 2 Kings, chapter 19, verses 35 through 37. Now Isaiah chapter 64, verse 4 states, "For from of old they have not heard nor perceived by ear, neither has the eye seen a God besides thee, who acts in behalf of the one who waits for Him." Seven hundred years before Christ it is written that until you know God, you cannot know Him, understand Him, know what He has waiting to give you or what He has predestined for your future. Christ spoke it as an absolute, and confirmed it an absolute when Christ repeated the written word. As we study the path to spirituality and our future changes, time passes on. Time and changes in our life run parallel to each other, sometimes immersing and sometimes parting. And as time never stops, this is an absolute, neither does the fact that your life changes also. Like it or not, it's changing by the minute and this is also an absolute.

In your Bible, turn to the Book of 1 Corinthians, chapter 2, verse 14. In the old version, "the unspiritual man does not receive the gifts of the spirit of God, for they are folly to him and he is not able to understand them because they are spiritually discerned." The new version from the American Standard Bible (verse 14) on the other hand states, "But a natural man does not accept the things of the spirit of God; for they are foolishness to him and he cannot understand them, because they are spiritually appraised." So can it be much plainer, how much plainer does it need to be? Unless we see and understand the knowledge of spirituality, we will walk in our sin nature or human nature as some call it until we make a choice, stay as I am or change. Stay as the person I have to act like every day or change and be the person I really am, even if I don't know myself—I still want to be me.

And so we open the door to the spirit world a little wider. The world of the unseen spirit. So many times we stand some distance away from our subject matter and see only the vague outline of its meaning, as we study further we can find the meaning to that which we have already read or consumed. As a man stands in an open field looking toward the forest, seeing the forest from a distance and its vast tree line along the edge of his open field, he may say to himself, "Now I have seen the forest." Now he returns to his people and says, "I have been to the forest and seen it, there is nothing to it just a bunch of trees." And they believe him and go on with their lives and their work. And so it is spiritually; we hear it but it passes by unknown. So let's step inside the forest, walk into the vague meaning of its depth. See the giant oaks, trees that have been here for hundreds of years, the maples that have such brilliant colors in the fall as the leaves turn from life to death. The ferns, the pines green and tall, the ground cover, the animals that live here, life beyond the reach of the man's mind that stood in the field and only looked toward the forest and not into it, and he said, "I have been there, there's nothing to it." We, you and I, now step a little closer to see the actual work in progress of the spirit world. Don't stand afar off, see its outline and say, "There's nothing to it, I've been there, believe me there is nothing there," "Been there, done that." Right! The blind leading the blind.

In our spiritual walk, we must continue with our observation into the transfiguration of Christ on Mount Tabor. Christ in His human form walks up the mountain, He has three men with Him, and they follow Him up until they all stop. Now we are walking into the forest, you and I. We now start to look at the individual trees and their structure. We have entered their world. Now be careful, don't let me lose you, don't become confused and get lost in this tangle of leaves and brush on the forest floor. This is going to be kept simple, one step at a time. "It's easy to get lost and confused in here." As was stated before, Christ in His human nature, He walks up the mountain. Now He, Christ, stops and changes into His divine nature. Matthew chapter 17, verse 1, says, "And six days later Jesus took with Him Peter and James and John and led them up to a high mountain by themselves." And verse 2 states, "And He was transfigured before them; and His face shone like the sun and His garments became as white as light." In verse 3, "And behold Moses and Elijah appeared to them, talking with Him." So now we see Christ leading in His human nature three men (in their human nature) and going up the side of the mountain. Simple, right? Now Christ stops and he becomes transfigured, meaning He, Christ, becomes spiritual. He comes into His divine nature, and is seen talking to two men. Christ in His divine nature is sinless. His face shines like the sun, His clothes turn a brilliant white, as white as light. Now we, you and I, see Christ in two natures: one His human nature like us, one His divine nature as God in the spirit.

We must in our spiritual walk of going in and coming out understand the two natures of Christ. Because if you and I do not understand His nature at the time of His life spent here on earth, then how can I say, "I understand," when I really don't. "I'm sure you have never done that before." Christ in His divine nature or being is God. Period! So let's start with His divine nature, because this is by far the ultimate, powerful, and sinless nature of God. In this divine nature of God is His divine will.

So as not to be confused by the forest, let's look at each tree individually, and by learning their characteristics, we can understand their place and how the forest functions around their presence.

Now look at God's will. Let's call it a property. We take God's divine nature and separate for a brief moment His divine will from His divine nature. Now we have two properties: one, His nature or who He is, and two, we have His will or His purpose of who He is and later his divine energy and how it affects us. "Our Father who art in heaven, hallowed be thy name, thy kingdom come, thy will be done, on earth as it is in heaven" (Matt. 6:9–10; the Lord's Prayer).

The will of God is His desire, or His choice, his deliberate action, His intention to express Himself in taking that action. But never must this will be of a demand and absolute, bound by the heavy chains of necessity. It must be a free will, to love, to desire, to be an active choice in the nature of its being.

So God's will is a free will, within His nature.

Now to say His nature is divine and to say His will is divine makes up two properties of who He is. This should be something we can understand. To go further into His nature, God has His divine energy. It is by this spiritual divine energy that all things were created. All men are healed and some have been raised from the dead. Some call it divine power. He, the Holy Spirit, comes with divine energy to help us, those that believe in Christ, to help us in our daily lives. In Mark 5:29–30, it states, "And immediately the flow of her blood was dried up and she felt in her body that she was healed of her affliction. And immediately Jesus, perceiving in Himself that the power proceeding from Him had gone forth, turned around in the crowd and said 'who touched my garments?'" This is the divine energy or power that we must understand. Because God in His awesome power shakes mountains by His presence, and the Scriptures state, "All knees shall bow" (Phil. 2:9 and 10), "in heaven and on earth." This should show us the nature of God, the will of God in that nature and the energy of that nature available to us, from God at His liking, His willingness, His very being.

Since He, our Lord Jesus Christ, is the son of God, He also is of the divine nature of God.

> All things have been given to me by my Father. (Matt. 11:27)

> All authority has been given to me by my Father. (Matt. 28:18)

> If you had known me you would have known my Father also. From now on you know Him, and have seen Him. (John 14:7)

AM I THE ONE YOU ARE LOOKING FOR?

> Believe me that I am in the Father and the Father in me. (John 14:11)

So now you can see the Trinity all in one, because the creator God, the Son Lord Jesus Christ, the Holy Spirit are all divine (sinless). All the same nature, same will, and same energy. God the Father, God the Son, God the Holy Spirit = the Trinity. All in one. So let us not be confused. God the Father's nature, will, and energy are not personal; they also belong to Christ and the Holy Spirit. This is why Christ and the Holy Spirit do the will of God, because His will is their will also, and their will is His will also. In Hebrews 10:9, Jesus said, "Behold I have come to do thy will, O God." Now, one more time! "Then God said let us make man in our image, according to our likeness" (Gen. 1:26). Then verse 27, "God created man in His own image and in the image of God He created them. Male and female He created them." So what does this tell us? What have you and I been missing of our past life? Why didn't someone explain this to me?

Don't just throw it out there to me and say you were made in God's image. So I go look in the mirror and all I see is me. I don't see God. So the first thing I say to the pastor teaching the lesson is, "Oh, now I understand." Sure I do! I was like the man standing in the open field looking off to the forest, only I couldn't even see the tree line. Of course I did not understand, but I'm not going to tell them that. Sure would make me look stupid if everybody else is nodding their head and saying, "Oh, yes, I understand." So let you and I now look at this in a simple spiritual way. We know God in His spiritual divine nature is not visible or touchable and that alone is a hidden property, hard for some of us to understand. But maybe we will hopefully sooner. Then later the creation of Adam, remember when we first started these writings and we looked at the egg. The shell was our sinful nature or physical nature. The egg white and the yolk was the will and souls spiritual self. So we came into this world with our human nature, our own free will, and our own spirit or energy. We are made in His, God's, image. Their image—the Father, the Son, and the Holy Spirit, the Trinity. But one thing: they are divine, sinless; we are sinful and corrupt.

But before the fall of Adam and Eve, we were also of the divine nature, only human. Visible and touchable. Because man disobeys God's spiritual laws, he becomes contaminated by evil, which is a direct confrontation to Him who is sinless and hates evil. As stated before, evil is disobedience, to disobey God's spiritual laws. Now let us look at Christ's human nature, born of a mother, raised as a child and became an adult. Look for yourself at His human nature. In Matthew 4:2 He became hungry, John 4:6 shows exhaustion, Luke 6: 12 shows a need for fellowship with God, in Matthew 9:36 he feels compassion for other people, and in Matthew 26:38 he is overwhelmed to the point of death. All of these verses and more are proof of His humanity, His human nature. Christ in His human nature inherited all of humanity's physical weaknesses and our limitations. But at the same time He also keeps His spiritual sinless nature, His divine nature. This is why He has two natures.

Why are we spending time and energy on this subject when we could be digging deeper into the spiritual realm? Because to go into and come out of their world, you and I must have the knowledge and wisdom and also the protection of Christ through God Almighty. You and I must know Christ and the hows and whys related to His divine nature, His deity. How do you expect to know who you are in your soul's self if you cannot confront the very being that has had you pretending to be the person you are not? They hide in plain sight. It was my ignorance of them that destroyed my life.

We are here to change, make a change, slight or not, maybe just a little change, maybe a big change.

It's your willingness to confront the voice that says put this book down, don't read any further, it's not true, this is trash talk; on and on and on. If you don't think that I don't hear this same voice as I write, think again. What am I doing writing this book, on this subject? No formal education, no IQ to speak of. Very low, if any, can't spell, can't organize my subject matter, an ex-alcoholic with his brains fried, for sure all of these things. For those of us in this position, we all are filthy rags, as far as the world is concerned. But not as Christ is concerned, remember He said to the thief on the cross, "Truly I say to you, today you shall be with me in Paradise" (Luke 23:43). One of the first to enter with Christ into His kingdom was a thief. This is why this book is written, not for those that know everything, or think they are beyond the spiritual laws of God, but for us who flounder and suffer in our life. The good, the bad, and the ugly. We all need to know the truth. In John 18:37 Christ said, "I have come into the world to bear witness to the truth. Everyone who is of the truth hears my voice."

There for you and I who want the truth shall find it with Him, Jesus Christ, and Him only.

In looking at the human nature of Christ, we see He is physical, has a will, soul, and has spiritual energy. In Hebrews 10:9 Jesus said, "I came to do your will O God." Christ in His human nature stands before us in this verse showing His human form or nature, "He comes to do." He is coming to do something. His human will, the property that we all have and freely born, with is wanting to do what God's spiritual will wants him to do. So we know that Christ is continuous in His life on earth to do what the Father wants. His will must be done according to Christ as He lived among us. In Mark 4:39 Jesus arose and rebuked the wind and said to the sea, "Peace, be still," and the wind stopped and the sea calmed: the waters became calm and the wind stopped. His voice, being human, commands nature to "be still." This shows His divine nature, His divine will, and His divine energy at work. He commands as a human being and nature obeys. This shows us that His divine nature and His human nature work in harmony with each other. One does not contradict the other. His divine will, a property that has command over divine energy, is in parallel with His human will and energy, which is our soul's makeup. So as He, Christ, enters into our soulish spiritual self, He brings with Him that divine energy and we now become energized with His sinless divine spiritual energy. This is our conversion taking place within us.

As we spoke of before when we pray the Lord's Prayer, "Your kingdom come, Your will be done on earth as it is in Heaven." What I'm saying to God is my will, my human willingness to follow whatever His will has for me to do I will do it on earth as it comes out of the heavens, and as I accomplish this work on earth willingly, spiritually, it has been accomplished in heaven before God's throne. How many times have you prayed this prayer in monotone and never have you ever thought to do His will after you said you would. Sure I said, "Thy will be done," and I went right out and did everything that I wanted to do. And when I failed I blamed it on someone else. It wasn't my fault; I'm not responsible for that. More bad luck. Did I do it with God's will, my will, and His will in harmony? Of course not! I just said I would, I don't have to do it, do I? "Sound familiar." The lips say one thing, the soul does another. And the same old question is asked. Well, I don't know His will, he doesn't talk to me. "I don't believe God talks to people." And the same old irresponsible excuses expounding from our mouths bring the same old repeated failures plus out of the unbelief, the refusal to believe in spiritual laws, the denial, to believe in God's will as a pathway to our life with peace and fulfillment with His protecting us from the very evil we bring upon ourselves through our unbelieving nature!

Visualize yourself in an open field, standing in its center, from all sides or edges of this field, is darkness. The arrows and darts begin to fill the air around you. You have no place to hide, no place to run to. Out of the darkness from all sides the projectiles fly, pointed at you; some miss, some hit, some hurt, but not too bad. Some of the darts and arrows that do hit in sensitive areas of your being causes great pain and suffering. Exposed to this destructive spiritual force day after day after day takes its toll on our life, weakens our resolve, weakens our resilience, and as we grow older, our age inhibits our movements. We cannot dodge the situations and the failures. It seems as though the arrows and darts are increasing as my aging continues and my failing health is pounded by circumstances that I cannot control, that I cannot understand. "Why me?" The question that you continually ask yourself, "Why me?" Isn't there anything or anyone out there to stop me from this continuous pounding by these unmitigated circumstances? The answer is "no." *Webster's Dictionary* explains "unmitigated" as an absolute, a suffering, not lessened or eased. As long as we live outside of God's will and place for us in His kingdom, you and I will not have a place to hide, a place of protection, the projectile hurled at us from the evil that the darkness holds and is polluted with; their home is outside the kingdom, outside of God's will for His people. If we live outside of God's kingdom in what is described as "the world," then we must and will receive what the unclean spirits, the fallen angels, governed by Satan that which he and his evil beings have in store for us. Now all of the denial from all of the people, rich and poor, educated and undereducated, whoever, wherever, must be put aside. For everyone who lives outside of God's will lives in the will of him and them that deceived Adam. To change your life from who you are acting like to the person you really are, you must leave that "world" and move. No matter how painful, no matter what today's circumstances are, you must move into "God's" kingdom. Remember, we are writing these things to prove to you the ability to change is available to those of you who want change. Again I say this is "not written for you who do not want to change your life, who want to stay in the world." In this book, not one time do I bring condemnation on anyone person who does not believe what is written here on these pages. It is your choice, your will shall be done in your life as you see fit. But because life is constantly changing, you may see what is available someday, down the road of detours and stop signs, green lights and red lights, black top highways and dirt roads. One thing never changes. The spirit world, God's kingdom, God's word, His promise to protect you and keep you forevermore!

So that we do not lose our place in the vast forest of spirituality, we look at the path before us. We see God the creator who created man in His image. Remember when He said, "Let us make man in Our image." So we were made with body, soul, and spirit. A human sinless nature of divine qualities, making us sinless and spiritual. And in Genesis chapter 1 verse 28, God blessed them, male and female, and said to them, "Be fruitful and multiply, replenish the earth and subdue it." If you read the following verses, you can see God giving man total control over all things, plants and animals, with His blessings over all of the earth. This was God's original will, for us to be like Him. It was His will, His own personal property of spiritual magnitude, His greatness, His divine energy, His grace, given to us to keep and have complete control over all things given to us by Him, our creator, our God over all things large and small—from the animal kingdom down to the smallest herb. We, you and I, could have control. That of course also means our life and our lifestyle as long as it was within his spiritual kingdom. "As long as it was all within His spiritual kingdom." How many times must we read this sentence? Read and repeat, repeat, repeat as long as I am in the will of God and in His spiritual kingdom I am safe, at peace, have abundance, with love for and forever, Amen.

Because man rebelled against the spiritual laws of God, he, man, walked out of God's kingdom into the kingdom of darkness. In verse 22 in chapter 3 of Genesis, the Lord said, "Because now man knows good and evil [both sides] he might eat from the tree of life and live forever." So this is proof that you and I, if we could eat from the tree of life, we could live forever. But because God knows we will now have an evil nature, a sinful nature given to us by Satan, He cannot allow us to live forever. Death now stands at the door as we enter into the kingdom of darkness, separating us from God. Who is death? Where does he come from? Is death a being of some kind? Is death an "it," or is death just a word, describing the end of life, period? If death has now entered into this conversation and it's just a word, describing the end of one's life, then why does death bring this feeling that rises up from our inward being? "Be careful," you're talking about man's death. Death says, "I hold the key to your existence," and an uncomfortable feeling generates in us to stop this conversation. You think maybe he just heard his name and he comes slithering out from the darkness to stop our perception of who he might be and to limit our knowledge of his presence in our life. Something to think about.

Let's go back to the tree of life and see what we can salvage from the absolute destruction that was brought upon mankind at that fateful day or time. Remember man's sinless nature before the snake, because this is important. Man's sinless nature had the power, the energy, the ability to have complete control over all things. His nature was human and divine. His will was with God and God's will. His spiritual nature was with God, complete contact with the Almighty as they walked through the garden together. The snake comes, calls on his unclean fallen one, "temptation," and Adam falls out of the will of God. Struck by the snake, filled with his evil venom, Adam now in chains, spiritually, has fallen.

For how many hundreds of years man is out of the will of God. We know from the Old Testament about man's rebellion against God's will and spiritual laws that man must obey without reasoning and constantly denying God's presence in our life. Now comes Christ, sent by the Father to give those that want a second chance to commune with God spiritually, to receive His divine energy, "grace" as we know it, and His divine nature to help us to become more divine in our nature. It's so very simple it's almost unimaginable, for us, you and I, to be like Him, talk to Him, and walk with Him. You're like Him when you obey His word and stay in His will, your prayers are like incense going up to Him in such sweet fragrance. Your presence with Him each day is walking with Him through your lifetime.

When I was an alcoholic and followed the addiction road to destruction, I knew denial, temptation, lust, carnality, depression, filth, unwashed, lowlife degenerate. So what! Leave me alone. As you set in your own spiritual and sometimes physical jail cell, you can contemplate where you are and who you are. I think some of us fall into this verse out of the Old Testament, the Book of Job, chapter 19 verses 10–11.

> He hath destroyed me on every side and I am gone: and mine hope hath he removed like a tree. He hath also kindled His wrath against me, and he counteth me unto Him as one of His enemies.

In my pride and arrogance before my fall, I was the giant oak, the hard core, hard to the bone. Did I listen to my wife, my elders, my friends, people trying to help me? Absolutely not. Who do they think they are? Their answers are certainly not my answers. "Go and get counseling," "I will not!" On and on and on, same old sounds, remember the old Victrolas that had records that played over and over, and when a record would crack or break and the needle hit the crack in the record, it made you jump up to shut it off. That same old sound over and over, it gets tiresome. The same old excuses played over and over because the person does not have control of his or her life. It's tiresome. Job says, "And God removes us like a tree that has been cut down. Destroyed on all sides." Job says, "I feel like God's wrath is coming against me and I know He sees me as one of His enemies."

The advice from my wife and my friends is what we might call unwanted and unsolicited. It was in those days I began to lose control; all is lost, everything is gone. Run, run and as fast as you can, but you cannot run fast enough or far enough. The demon is with you. You cannot outrun the very one who has control of you. In Job, chapter 21, verse7, it says, "Wherefore do the wicked live, become old, and yes are mighty in power." In this conversation Job is having with his friends, Job explains how some people go a full lifetime without the Lord, without God. For they in their abundance, Job says, spend their days in wealth, their houses are safe and the rod of God is not upon them; they the unbelievers and their children dance to the sound of the timbre and the harp and they rejoice at the sound of the organ. Even their animals give birth without having any trouble at all. What are they doing right and what am I doing wrong that such calamity falls on me and not on them? This question is asked many times in some men's lives. Be careful here. This is ground on the forest floor that we walk on. Thinking we are always on a solid, firm foundation when underneath the leaves and grass is a pit, dug by the trapper, the old sly one, the demon who says why can't you be like her, why can't you be like him?

When we are contemplating the idea in our mind we want to make a change in our life, be careful! Who are you going to follow? You must have some idea of someone you want to be like, some other place you would like to be. Someone else you want to be with. This is not some heavy-duty psychological programming. Come on! We all think these things some of us actually try to act them out. And some of us actually end up in the pit. Now that I have fallen into the pit, I still obey the very voice that put me there and he says, dig deeper, work harder so you can get yourself out of this hole. Stop and have a drink, smoke a joint, snort a little, shoot up, on and on, deeper and deeper, there is no bottom. Just darkness, getting darker and darker. In the Book of Romans chapter 1, verse 22, I find a good picture of myself as I see now who I was then. "Professing themselves to be wise, they became fools!" There is no one, none, not anyone living or dead that can change your life except Christ. Do not expect other religions to deliver you from your bondage, whatever it might be. Ask yourself, do I pray to a dead man who still lies in His grave, his bones turning to dust in the depth of complete darkness in the bowels of the earth? What is he going to do for you? Is their god made of wood, stone, an animal, or part of the earth? What can these properties do for us if they all were created by the God of heaven? He created all of these things, and now because I want to see what I'm praying to, I bypass the creator, turn my back on Him to pray to His creations.

As Paul writes many times in the New Testament, "May it never be!" This book is not written to dissect other religions. But never forget, "Their God is not my god." Do not believe those that say, "Oh, we all believe in the same God, He just has different names." "May it never be!" Christ with His two natures, one divine spiritual nature and one sinless human nature, is the only human being that walked this earth and returned to earth in His spiritual nature by walking through closed doors and then became human, in His nature to prove to mankind He is the son of God, the creator of old.

In your New Testament Bible, read John 20:19–29. It confirms His spiritual to human in natures or beings. In verse 27 Christ in His human nature said, "Reach here your finger and see my hand and put your finger into my side and be not unbelieving but believing." Verse 29 also says, "Because you have seen me have you believed? Blessed are they who did not see and believed."

Chapter 10
The Church

So this group of men, closed up in a room, afraid for their very lives, and through the locked doors and walls that these men found safety in, out of the spiritual, unseen nature or form Christ passes through the door and walls into their presence. He does not have to change His spiritual nature. He, Christ, could have been there unseen in their presence for a long time, listening to their conversations, watching their actions. He didn't have to and was not bound by obedience to come into His human form. He changed into His human nature or form or property, whatever. Because of His willingness to prove to mankind He was human, but also spiritual—two natures. Then He said, "Do you believe me, have you believed." Now He says blessed are they that have not seen, who did not see, and yet believe. You and I did not see and so that blessing we did not and cannot receive. But you and I can believe in Christ spiritually, without seeing Him in His human nature, and can receive His blessings of His divine nature. There are many ways and many teaching in our "Christian churches" today.

So as not to point fingers at anyone or his or her denominations, because first, Christ is our life-changing experience and only Him, later comes the Church. I'll sure catch flack for that statement, but since I'm just a layperson and not schooled in long words and deep knowledge, I think the question has been asked many times, was the church created for Christ or did Christ come for the church?

From the Scriptures I believe Christ came for you and me, we, lay people, Gentiles, pagans, Hebrews, and from all walks of life and from rich, poor, wanted, unwanted, from the roadsides and bedsides, from all over the world we came. We came into our enclosures, our room, our buildings for our protection, for our safety, from the catacombs beneath the ground's surface to the most beautiful gold-and-silver-layered cathedrals did we come. We came because we believed in the spiritual nature of His spiritual presence in these places later to be called churches. We came and still come to this day to be blessed and want our continued divine energy, our in-filling, like a fuel needed so we can do the will of the one who blesses us with the very energy it takes to walk each day of our life. And while we are on the subject of churches, we can discuss our pastors, our priests, our bishops, cardinals, our patriarchs, our theologians. All men of God, schooled to lead us, help us to understand the Scriptures, promote well-being in the churches, settle our disagreements, and continually help us recommit, reunite, help us in our repentance of our sins and pray for us each day, as we and they, our spiritual leaders, try to walk the path of righteousness each day in a world of sin, carnality, and turmoil. But if any would someday read this writing, you who lead us, you who have been schooled in biblical teaching, do not look down on your laypeople. Do not say to yourself you know more than they. We came and still come to church to find Christ, not to come to see and hear how great you are.

I came to Christ two years before I ever entered a church. I read and read and read. I read the history of the church from the apostles, many of the holy fathers of each century since Christ, great men and women who in every century have made the church greater in her ability to feed the flock spiritually. Why wasn't I told about the great men and great women who gave up their lives so that I, you and I, could be freed from the very demons that almost destroyed my life? And today, this very day, are destroying lives over all this earth. Some pastors condemn the teachings of other churches. I have known pastors to laugh at the teaching of Mary, mother of God. Being a virgin after giving birth to Christ, "she had a baby, she can't be a virgin, how dumb can you be son?" When I asked them about this same Scripture we just read about Christ passing through shut doors and walls spiritually and then becoming human, why Christ could not spiritually pass through the birth canal and not break the seal of Mary's womb, enter into her arms as a child? From this question I get a dumb stare. And no answer. Why didn't some of these great theologians tell me as a young man that men that gave their life to Christ and made a life following His spiritual laws and spiritual ways died and were buried and hundreds of years later by coincidence were dug up to be moved and found their bodies to be the same as when they were buried hundred years before. They call it an incorruptible body.

Well, come to find out that the divine nature of Christ who comes to live in us at the time of our conversion will by God's grace "divine energy" clean our soul and bodies of our corruptible nature. As we go deeper into Christ, we become more divine, and more pure energy is given to us as we progress spiritually. I didn't know that. These bodies are in churches to this day. Read about it. It mattered not what their past was; it only mattered what they did with their lives after their conversion, leaving the spirit of darkness who controls the world's society and enters into the light of Christ through commitment and discipline. Now His divine nature becomes the master of our soul. Not the garbage thrower and his demoniacs. To end this conversation on belief and the power of God against other beliefs, I want you to read the Book of Romans chapter 1, verses 28–32. "And even as they did not like to retain God in their knowledge, God gave them over to a reprobate mind, to do things that are not convenient" (v. 28). What this means, it means that Christ will give your mind over to the other guy, you know, the one who lives down under. What does reprobate mean? Webster says it means unprincipled; your mind will *not* be under your control. It will have no principles to guide your life. No standards, no ethics, it's corrupt. Verse 29 says, "filled with unrighteousness," means sinful, wicked, unfair. Your mind will be given to those spirits who will make you sinful, wicked, unfair, and unjust. Remember verse 28, your mind will be given over to all of these things. As we continue to unravel the mind's mysteries of why we do things we do not want to do, we are not talking about the world of psychiatry and treatments of the mind; this is left to those in their field of medicine. We are talking spiritual things, beings and powers that lead us where we do not want to go, and sometimes, where do we want to go? I'm not getting this information out of a medical journal. It's out of a book written over two thousand years ago, for all to see and understand. Nothing hard about that is there? Simple enough if you look at it through the doors of the spirit world. We are looking into their world, remember. Look at their ways, laws, or ordinances. An ordinance is a prescribed practice, a decree of fate, of a deity, could be a religious rite.

I'm sure that everyone who reads these notes knows far better than I the meaning of these words. My only interest is how they affect us spiritually as we walk each day down a spiritual path. Because I would not and did not acknowledge the Lord in my life, because I thought I was the only one, "It's all about me," not at all willing to share my life with His will so it could be convenient, so my life would be a life of a convenience to myself and others. No, I didn't want just a bite of Adam's apple, I wanted the whole tree. Sound familiar?

To go back to verse 28, because I did not retain, "to hold or to keep in mind, to keep in a fixed state, or continue to practice." To retain God in my knowledge He, the Lord, gave my mind to those that waited, some of whom I had already invited in, by my lifestyle, by my thinking, by my actions, and by my wanting to be someone I was not. The Lord in verse 29 gives my mind over to fornication.

Who's that? So what's the deal, the real deal? This is no biggie, just fornication. What's Webster say about fornication? He explains it this way. It is the act of intercourse between men and women both unmarried. If one is married it's adultery. Idols worshipped.

Chapter 11
Idols

It becomes an idol, it becomes a passion; the person loses control of his or her ability to keep their mind on anything but sexual desires. They continually are glorifying their own sexuality. Morals are cast to the wind, anything goes. Honor to your partner is for one night only if that. It seems as if they cannot be ever satisfied with their present partner. These people are under the spell of a passion they cannot control. If you are continually looking and feeding your mind and body with this lust to commit the acts of intercourse, you had better start to listen to the voice in your mind by stillness and discernment. The Lord can quench this fire raging within you. But only He can and will through prayer, humiliation toward God, invite His presence into each encounter with that demon of lust who, in the end, will, without the Lord, destroy your life. No matter how many affairs you have, the demon of lust cannot be satisfied. Remember, none of these spirits that come out of the darkness can be satisfied by our actions under their control. As you get older they get stronger, and you get weaker. It is only through the Lord do you find peace and sensibility, control and freedom from their assaults. Who are these people driven by lust? Why are they the way they are? And how can we see or discern this movement in that person or even in ourselves? Since we have spent time reading about the presence of Christ and His divine nature in our life, let us look now into the evil nature or properties of those that destroys our innocence, our peace, our blessings, and for some our very way of life, our soul. We talked earlier about Avarice, the demon of money. He is the one who locks our brain into a gear that propels us into thinking all things revolve around money, material objects, to a point we worship them or it. Some of them go so far as to commit suicide, to kill themselves, because they lose their material possessions. Nothing is spiritual about these idols, wood, stone, paper, gold, silver, metal, on and on. It's the feeling you get when you look at these material idols, the feeling that makes you love it, cherish it, talk to it. That feeling is spiritual, and don't let anyone, anywhere, any place tell you it is not. And they will and with great verbalization.

Remember back some pages ago we talked about stillness and its great power, simplicity and its great ability to keep us focused on our goals. Well, if you can, start to be still and quiet for a few moments and simply look at and observe your feelings at a given moment. You can and will discern who is causing this feeling or what is called a passion, and why is he or it making you do what you do. Because we all function on feelings and what later becomes a passion, because the exhilaration of that feeling as it continually grows, it causes us to be dumbfounded with all other things going on around us, if that passion becomes strong enough. This passion, driven by an unclean spirit who continually is wiping his filthy finger across your brain, will in time create the climatic ecstasy or a high beyond normal feeling. We've talked about this before.

Again we go back and look at what we have just read. We know that divine energy given to you and me comes from the Lord God Almighty, through Christ, by the Holy Spirit, to us. If this pure spiritual energy can be transfused into our soul so that we become stronger spiritually, gaining the strength to overpower our old habits and passions, it's all happening spiritually. Once our conversion to Christ becomes our cornerstone, the cornerstone of our temple being built in our soulish nature, this pure undefiled energy is available. Does heat warm the body on a cold winter day? For sure it will. It penetrates the body deep to our very bones. Does cool air refresh us on a steaming hot day? For sure it will. Heat and cold are outside forces of our natural being, our normal body temperatures. So spiritually we receive the holy energy as we receive the hot and cold elements, only with more forcefulness and longer lasting, it becomes a force in our inner self. It holds the truth of who we really are and works against vain imaginations. People without divine energy, without the infilling needed to support their defense mechanism, their spiritual power to control their passions, which works in the unseen world of the spirit, cannot and will not be in control of their life spiritually.

The Bible explains it very simply in the Book of Romans chapter 1, verses 21 and 22. Again we repeat, if you are to find yourself, who you really are, not denying and procrastinating, there is only one book that can help us in our spiritual journey. No other book in the history of mankind can give you and me the spiritual knowledge we need on our road to a greater life, a better life, a fuller life and beyond all things, peace and love. God grant you many years. This book is the Holy Bible.

> Because that they knew God they glorified Him not as God, neither were thankful; but became vain in their imaginations, and their foolish heart was darkened. Professing themselves to be wise they became fools. (Rom. 1:22–23)

The same demonic spirit that attacks a man today was and is the same spirit that caused men thousands of years ago to act the same way then. Nothing is changed. We die and pass away. It, the spirit, passes from one human being to another as the centuries come and go. The demon never changes. So like the unclean spirits that fuel our passions today, it was and has been the same throughout the past and will be in the future until a change in the spiritual environment occurs. They will continue to manifest themselves in our lives, bringing destruction, confusion, corruption, despondency, sickness, and addiction to many facets of our life. Verse 21 states that men that know God don't or will not glorify Him. You know, the guy or gal that laughs at your belief in the Lord. Their favorite saying is, "Oh, I know God, don't try to bring that junk over here. You people are sick with your religion," as we have stated before, on and on and on.

But they imagine themselves to be great, full of pride and vain words and thoughts. They are not thankful for the life they have been given and their ability to live each day, never thinking that spiritually they have and are following the creature and not the creator. Their heart, meaning their inner self, follows the darkness of the creature and pollutes the soul with evil energies, feeding the passions of unrighteousness each day, thinking this is "normal."

So in professing themselves to be great and so very wise and all-knowing (they continually try to impress us with their deep intellectual knowledge), they become fools. Why is it they try so hard to sell us their way of thinking? Why do they profess their way is the only way? Why when they themselves are being led into the darkness by those that live under the authority of the thief and the murderer? Our passion to be great and extraordinary has sold us out to an invisible devil. And to clarify myself in writing these notes, I do not in any way profess this is the only way for all men and women. I have stated before and will again, only those that want a change in their life, only those that want a soul change, a renewal of their soul, a manner of life that follows the pathway to truth, so we can imitate the heavenly beings, not those sent to us from the pit, finding peace in who we are.

It is by this divine energy that overpowers the demon, annihilating the passion that has put a hook in our jaw. Now divine energy can and will put us into a new spiritual realm. Now you can be who you are. Now you can be the person that God created, the real you. Now you can say "goodbye" to your old self.

When I was down, very far down in my life, when I had lost everything including the destruction of my soul, my marriage, my business, relationships with family and friends, when I laid flat on my back looking up then and only then did I start to ponder, why had this happened? When I finally sobered up and stood still long enough to admit to myself that I was the problem, I was my own worst enemy, I created this person, and there had to be a way out of this box, this pit fill of snakes and filth, this world I was living in had to change or death was certain and not far off. It was in those days I searched for the clues to lead me up and out of my box. After reading articles on spirituality, I started to become more and more curious as to the causes and effects of spiritual discipline, not thinking only but doing and continually watching myself. I think psychology 101 calls it introspection, to look inside yourself. We all hear voices; we all obey one voice or another.

Your thinking is a voice. Your conscience, if you have one, is a voice. Most of the time it's a whisper, your brain lies to you every day, sometime or another. We all have a conscience, but some of us shut it down and some even deny its existence. Some of us never think of our brain being a voice, but think about it. If you are controlled by what you think, how about who controls what you think about. How much plainer can it be? We were reading a few pages back a while ago and we talked about simplicity and how important it was in our spiritual walk to keep things simple and understandable. Have you ever been so engrossed in what your brain is telling you and you're listening so intently you drive your car halfway across town and you can't remember ever going past a stop street or stopping for a traffic signal? You go to do something and by the time you're ready to do it, you have forgotten what you're supposed to be doing. It's all because you had other things on your mind. Certainly, you were listening to your familiar voice, just you and him. No one knows what you are thinking, what the voice is saying, and what you are responding to or how you are going to respond, no one except you and the voice, your brain power.

How about who controls what you think with. What if an unknown property has control of what you think and how you think. That unseen being or property can control you if it can control your brain. You're thinking that you respond to every hour of every day of your life. Now who is in control: you, it, or them? Let us look to the Old Testament to find an example of today's feelings, society's feelings, not only the secular or nonbelieving environment but also the sometime Christian walk. This particular segment or door we are about to open will shed some darkness and some light on the feeling of today's world. The same "feeling" that has been passed to generation to generation to generation for thousands of years. Remember the people feel and act basically the same then as they do today. Why? Would it be the same spirits or spirit who never change in their unholy self-esteem that become so familiar in our life we do not notice them or notice the change in our nature as we drift more and more toward their way or ways, on our constant rush to succeed, and have more and more material possessions?

Isaiah chapter 47, verse 10 says, "And you felt secure in your wickedness and said 'no one sees me' your wisdom and your knowledge, they have deluded you.' For you have said in your heart 'I am' and there is no one besides me." Wickedness is expressed by what you and I do to other people in the form of harming them. By acts of dishonesty, theft, oppression, fraud, violence, and extortion, violating God's standards for the treatment of others. Remember we said in earlier writings on the subject of sin. All sin involves some violation of the divine standard of God. Wicked in its translation focuses on some of these or all standards. So the Lord said you have trusted in your own wickedness. Meaning you have no respect for other people's feelings for one, you and I, we can do and act in whatever manner we want to just as long as it gets us what we want, when we want it.

Honoring someone else's feelings or property is not our problem. You have to do what you have to do to get ahead. If they get in your way, well, too bad. Just walk on by and leave them in your dust. Who cares about God's standards anyway. Most of us don't even know what they are and could care less. We are busy, can't you see, I don't have time.

The Lord continues. Your wisdom and your knowledge has perverted you. *Webster's New World College Dictionary* explains "perverted," deviating from what is right or good or true. Misdirected, corrupted, misinterpreted, distorted. So your own personal wisdom and knowledge has perverted you? How can that be? Remember we talked about wisdom before. It's the ability to make the right choices, the right judgment calls, that is spiritual wisdom. By divine energy, God's grace, you receive this gift by obeying His standards, your fear of His retribution if you continue to sin. The world's wisdom, that is yours and mine without God is that this is all foolishness. Remember two entirely different wisdoms: one is God's spiritual wisdom, implanted in us by His choice, the other is our wisdom, by human nature only and implanted by the world, which is shallow and perverted, and given to us by the world. Paul writes in Corinthians 1:26, "There are not many wise according to the flesh," and if we are worldly, then for sure we are fleshly. So by our own sin nature, the wisdom and knowledge we have comes to the conclusion, "I AM THE GREAT I AM," and there is no one else but me.

So that we won't be led in the wrong direction as some are going to say about these writings, let us look at who this is written and spoken of. Isaiah 47:1 to the Chaldeans: Who were they? They were a tribe from southern Babylon, they were Babylonians. They were an educated class of advisers and administrators in Babylon and later empires of the Middle East. They were astrologers and astronomers, priests. In the years 640–609 BC, in your Old Testament Bible, Habakkuk chapter 1, verse 6, "For behold I am raising up the Chaldeans," God said then and later in Isaiah He admonishes them for their actions; evil will come upon them. I have used this example of the Chaldeans because it dates back long before Christ, but yet shows us the reaction God has when our thinking and our actions stray from His spiritual laws or standards. As we continue to study the Bible as it progresses toward our times today, we have learned nothing about spiritual living. Because the people thought they were so great, so educated, so wise, so knowledgeable that they could walk in their own known vainglory. They knew it, and so do we. Look at history and see the downfall of great men because they said, "I AM." We limp, not walk. Today, look around you at the proud look. I was there. I was wrapped up tight in vanity and pride. I know how it feels. And today I know who that feeling is.

You know that old saying, "Well, I can identify with that." The same can be said about our feelings. Stop and listen, be still. Hear his voice? This is a bunch of garbage, put the book down, burn it, you don't have time for this, Dullsville!

The demon spirit "Vainglory" speaks. For our reference we are using *The Ladder of Divine Ascent* by Saint John Climacus. There are many forms of evil, but evil is evil, and so it is with vainglory. To begin with vainglory is a change of nature, meaning this is not our normal or natural way of life; we are not born this way, but could be brought up this way in our adolescent years, but mostly we acquire the demon as we become more successful. He perverts our character and is a child of the spirit of unbelief. If at one time you believed, became successful, because the Lord gave you out of His abundance, and you said, "I have made myself rich," or, "I have made myself beautiful," or any virtue given to you by the Spirit of the Lord and because you feel so good about yourself your unbelief now starts to be more and more stronger. "I don't need God, look what I have done, and look, what is this great future I have because I am so great." In the Old Testament (American Standard Version), Solomon writes in the Book of Proverbs, chapter 26, verse 12. "Do you see a man wise in his own eyes? There is more hope for a fool than for him." Same Proverbs older translation (King James Version) chapter 26, verse 12 states, "Seest thou a man wise in his own conceit? There is more hope of a fool than of him." Explanation, from Charles Bridges 1794–1869, of Proverbs, The Geneva Series of Commentaries, "God means to point His finger at this man," "see him." "The man holds himself fit to be a standard for other folks to live by." He holds himself wise because he knows not what it is to be wise. And yet how strangely does the smallest amount "puff up" and fill a man full of himself.

Paul writes in Romans chapter 12, verse 16, "Be not wise in your own conceits." Now for us to be very much aware of vainglory, be aware because if you think you are wise and great, your mind is lying to you and you are holding a delusion in your hand, a shadow that you think is substance. Multitudes have mistaken this feeling for an everlasting moment, only to find if not soon enough, if not rectified in time, it will be the ruination of your soul for eternity.

Does it ever seem in our rush to be somebody, to act like who we think we should be, to go daily trying to "put on the dog," "run a fast tractor," be number one, everybody wants to be "number one," right? Did it ever occur to you that you are knocking at the wrong door? St. John Climacus writes, "It is a great work to shake from the soul the praise of men, but to reject the praise of demons is greater." "It is very difficult to drive away a hungry dog from a butchers counter." In our Christian walk, many times we think we are so much better than those we consider "unsaved." Well, well, who do you think it might be that speaks to us and says, "Set out now in order to save the souls which are perishing"? Like a man in a restaurant said to his friends as he got up to leave, "I've got to go, I've got to go downtown and save a bum. Maybe I'll get lucky and save two or three." Lord have mercy on his soul. You cannot serve two passions at the same time, so as we will see in these next writings, pride moves in, for pride is the consummation of vainglory. The feeling of vainglory is the "knowing feeling." I know, I know, I just want to display all of my knowledge for the benefit of the people within hearing range and those that see me. In his writings St. John Climacus says and to my question, "How is vainglory the mother of pride? Pride the demon spoke and said 'praises exalt and puff one up:' and by Vainglory the soul is exalted, the demon Pride seizes the soul, lifts it up to heaven and then casts it down into the abyss. Destruction awaits." Lord Jesus Christ, Son of God, have mercy on my soul, a sinner.

As we look through the open door to the spiritual world, we see what is the beginning for us as far as understanding is concerned. But for them, those angelic beings that were cast down from heaven and have followed Satan since that time and will continue to do his work as long as God permits, they are thousands of years old, nothing new about them and their work, it's just a mere mention in today's society. Here we are now, one step closer to the opening and we see vainglory. Let's look at it as a property, a being, more than a substance, not a shadow, not a mist, but the invisible property of a spirit. Vainglory wants to and begs to be given the first place in the choir, or the first place at the table. Vainglory, that abominable demon, suggests that we should pretend to have some virtue that we do not possess. Why? Because if we are worldly, we want everyone to speak "about how great I am," telling how great we are. If we are religious, then Vainglory quotes Scripture to us and says, "Follow me; you great and wonderful thing." "Let your light so shine before men that they may see your good works" (Matt. 5:16).

There has been much written on the subject, "Can a Christian have a demon?" We are not going to argue this subject. So that we are not left with vague and lack of definite understanding, we should spend one moment to clarify the question. Place Christian standards at the top of the pinnacle, place the people who try to live by these standards daily and try to work out their salvation on a daily basis with a commitment to Christ, but not only Christ but the Father

God, Christ the Son and Lord God, the Holy Spirit—the Trinity. For those with great minds and much more knowledge than mine, you go argue with the Scriptures. Christ said, "I do nothing without the Father" (John 12:49, Matt. 10:40, Luke 10:16, Eph. 4:30), and do not grieve the Holy Spirit (Luke 12:12) for the Holy Spirit will teach you in that very hour what to say. Luke 10:21, at the very time, He rejoiced (He meaning Christ) greatly in the Holy Spirit and said, "I praise thee O Father Lord of heaven and Earth that thou didst hide these things from the wise and intelligent [worldly] and didst reveal them to babes." Those that receive divine grace the babes were the seventy men that He, Christ, had sent out to do His work and returned to tell Christ, "Even the demons are subject to your name" (Luke 10:17). Enough said, but one last clue for those that are so learned and for us who are being laughed at by you, as your words send the spirit of intimidation into our presence. In the New Testament, Mark 8:38, Christ speaks, "For whoever is ashamed of me and my words in this adulterous and sinful generation [today's generation], the Son of Man [Christ] will also be ashamed of him when He [Christ] comes in the glory of His Father and the holy angels." The whole message is not to become weak and relent to their unbelief and intimidation. With Christ in us, all demon spirits are subject to us when using the name of Jesus Christ. And don't forget it, ever! Be sure to continue to open your Bible to all of these Scriptures and read for yourself the book chapter and verse. I am not the authority; the I am, the "great I am" is the authority here. Let the Holy Spirit be your teacher. "Peace be unto you the reader, that the Holy Spirit gives you knowledge and understanding as He comforts you this day." "Lord Jesus Christ, Son of God, have mercy on me, a sinner."

Now let us return to our subject matter "vainglory," before he sneaks away and tries to escape from our probing and searching. Of all things they hate most is to be identified, to be seen. He would find it great for us to be found dozing away our time and energies, finding for us a false excuse why not to be on his trail. Since vanity wants us to pretend that we have some virtue that actually we do not possess, does it make us wonder how much more we pretend to be like someone else, or try to impress others with our worldly glory, hiding our own shameful thoughts and deeds that may cause others to stumble and fall spiritually? If you stand around and wait for someone to praise you, to say you're so wise and have such knowledge and intelligence, you're so well spoken, you have just been seduced by a demon. Don't read this message and then say, "I don't understand." You and I and all of us know that feeling of power and strength, that good feeling inside of ourselves, and can you get puffed up. Like a hot air balloon, you go straight up into the highs of heaven. But what about your fall—and you will—what about your soul; it knows who you really are, and it shrinks in horror because the fall is sure to come.

We just spoke of the demon Pride lifting our soul up and then casting it down. Remember the physical, the soulish, and the spirit. Three properties we are made of. Don't forget how these properties work in conjunction with each other. You and I may forget, but the demon does not. It's his existence; his existence is at stake here. He cannot live in our house when it is swept clean. He creates the confusion, the carnality, our sinfulness, the clutter of flattering displays of glorious worship, without faith and the passions. Your vanity now starts to control your thinking and the demon subdues your spirit entirely. It's your soul he wants. How long it takes is not an issue; he is thousands of years old, and time means nothing to him. But our time is short. We must not give up, stumble, yes, fall out of God's grace, yes. But not to give up and succumb to the demon's false praise and shallow gifts with no spiritual substance in any of his unholy palpitations he creates in our body.

The Lord waits for us to reclaim our position of authority over vainglory and pride. Our discipline and fortitude must, with God's help, prevail.

As vanity now controls our nature, our physical body, including the mind and our senses, we now become more judgmental, judging others' actions and decisions, thinking all of the time we have the answer. "You don't even have to ask me for an answer to your problem, I'll tell you what you should do anyway. I'll know if you like it nor not. If I insult you or hurt your feelings or bring depression on you, that's okay, as long as I can voice my opinion." This is now the beginning of insensibility. Once vainglory has found a room in your house and has a foothold, a position of praise, and you become obedient to wanting and receiving continuous praising and puffing up so that you can now expound the demons philosophy. He wipes his filthy finger across your brain and you feel his power, immediately you are a wise commentator, a person of great wisdom. "I am the I am, I am so beautiful." You are a self-contradictory windbag, you have become numb to the feelings of others, and you are a door to despair. Not only are you full of vanity and insensibility, but now the demon of pride has been invited into your house. Unknown to you he sits back in his chair and turns on the TV, watches the actions of the other two just mentioned, and he readies himself for the upcoming takeover of the person's mind. The person's soul and spirit has become imprisoned in the complete darkness that the demonic authority brings as it enters in and again we say, "The man or woman's state of being is worse now than it was before." The man that let's insensibility in without a fight is falling to a new low. Of course if you don't know or have spiritual knowledge, you can't fight the natural takeover of your body, soul, and spirit of these forces mentioned. So as vanity gives you a false high feeling, insensibility gives you a deadened feeling. When this spirit starts to turn up his power source, he is like the blind man who teaches others to see; the poor wretched man is not ashamed of his own words.

You or he hurts others around him and irritates us all with his condemnation of others who try to help those that are hurting. Your body struggles to get even more of this passion because the feeling of dominance over others is so strong. For you who have been and are caught up in the power play of these oh so familiar spirits, you will deny their presence in you. You will deny their existence, nevertheless being part of your life. Lord Jesus Christ, Son of God, have mercy on me, a sinner.

Stop and think. When have you gone to a funeral of a loved one, mourning their loss, while someone in the crowd can't wait to get to the food that is put forth after the service? How does this stony, obstinate raging stupid passion conquer our being, our natural God-given birthright to be loving, kind, humble, patient, and forgiving? By time and ignorance, the demon wins. The stinkpot demon of gluttony who has fathered the demons of vanity and insensibility is so strong in us that we want to eat, show everyone how much we can get on our plate, lean over the dish, fork in hand, and now "consume," never once even thinking of the dead, the death you know is not visible; your death is in not knowing your own ignorance of who is leading you to your death. If you are one of these people, the death you know is only caused by your inability to get the first chair at the head of the table, have everyone listen to your garbage mouth as you refill your plate for the second time. I should have discovered this stinkpot in me years ago. I was powerless to come against this sickness as many are today. But by knowledge of the Spirit can we start a reprogramming of our inner works. Now by the power of divine energy, God's grace, we can be set free from those that have their program ready to insert into our mind.

Have you ever watched some people in prayer, stony, hard, some even darkened? They sit or stand in the church, look at the altar, and feel nothing. When they take Communion, they act as if it's just ordinary bread. One man said to me once, "This is just grape juice, so what's the big deal."

"Insensibility is the good friend of a full belly," writes Saint John Climacus. But remember, someone who is insensitive—think about who you might know—this person is very caught up in sensual pleasures. If you are caught up in the passions of physical sensual pleasure and treat your targets with a mouth dripping with sugar, coated rat poison, an inner dominating resolution to conquer your target's resistance and relieve yourself of this desire, what you call bodily needs, you have just been had by insensibility and his buddy Lust. Two demons who have taken up residence in your house, daily they pound your conscience into submission, driving out all virtues you may have acquired before they came into you. And this is not all for you. Don't think you can escape, your other side will be seen.

The demons pick your targets for you. They tell you the targets' weak spots and how you can charm them into submission. But what about those that don't succumb to your false lies and find you disturbing and distrustful? Your treating of them is despicable, your whole nature changes, and you succumb to the very own beast with in you. Your flesh is insulted that he or she sees through you, and to protect the demons, you insult your target and try over a period of time to distract them or at the least make it difficult as possible for them. You are insensitive to the hurt and hardship you and the demons have brought upon the one who saw through your despicable action.

Our Lord never meant it to be this way. Our human nature was meant to love and care for each other. We must be sensitive to each other's suffering, not create even more, but heal the pain with everlasting soulish God's love, given to us by the Lord as a virtue, a gift, and this gift, this virtue now allows us to be who I really am. God's love allows us to desire Him more than we desire the flesh.

Let us long for God with all of our strength that we can be ourself and not the destroyer of this nature and life before us. Chasing after pleasures that in the end are resulting in great pain and everlasting spiritual annihilation. You and I must discipline our flesh, we must wash our soul clean and try every day to help someone—give to the poor, treat someone kindly, stay humble above all things—no matter how hard Vainglory and Insensitivity scream. Make yourself do these things. The soul will honor God-given virtues before it will cave into the now spiritual suffering flesh. The flesh must become the weaker voice. So spiritually cut his voice off entirely by obeying the Scriptures and thanking God our Lord Jesus Christ and the Holy Spirit for all the things in your life.

Your Bible, John 16, verse 33, Christ said, "These things I have spoken to you, that in me you may have peace. In the world you have tribulation, but take courage; I have overcome the world."

Remember when we first started this reading? And remember we said if you want to change, if you want to be who you were meant to be, not someone who every day has to put on his or her act for all of the world to see how great we are. But inside of ourself, our soul cries out in its weakness; we feel anxious and struggle to get through each day. Weak inside but trying desperately hard to cover it up by our intelligence, stimulated by our ignorance, lack of common sense, and having no spiritual knowledge, none! We force our bodies through one more day. Remember we said nothing can change you, no matter what you do if it's not spiritual. Then you will stay the way you pretend to be.

It is because you are part of the world. The worldly passion of self-love and all its desires. The Lord said, "In the world you have tribulation." What is tribulation? The *Revell Bible Dictionary* states tribulation as (1) pressures from enemies or circumstances, often as divine judgment; (2) deep emotional and spiritual distress caused by pressures from within or without. So if we are living in the world without Christ for our God and Savior, then the demonic behavior causes us to be pressured in circumstances that go against God's spiritual laws that have been in place since man was created.

Now emotional stress deep inside of ourselves builds. Spiritual distress now takes place because our nature does not and will not be totally consumed by evil. Our willingness to be free, our wanting to be free from them and their constant activity in us and around us, does at times break out and speak to us inwardly. My days as an alcoholic, my addiction to that and other vices put my spiritual distress to a new low. I remember clearly, "I hate myself. I hate who I have become." And that is what they do as long as they are in control. They, the demoniacs, have been doing their job since they fell out of heaven, so why have we put up with them? Our human sin nature, our flesh, we love it so! They wipe their filthy finger across our brain, giving us a sensual jolt, away we go, only to become more like them as we become weaker and they become stronger in our lives. We become old. Now we have become exhausted from our fight, if we did fight, and as the Scripture reads, "And when you become old they will come and lead you where you do not want to go." I'll give you a heads-up! This means spiritual, and don't let the naysayers tell you it's only physical. You ask them, "Who are they?" The Lord said, "That in Me you may have peace." So how complicated can this be? In Him, meaning spiritually, we have to be in Him; meaning we have to have Him as our Lord, which gives Him full authority over us, within and without. How can He promise me peace in my life when all of this time I have had tribulation, pain, and suffering? Because His promise is true, and the truth will set you free.

We talked about this transition from tribulation to peace. Remember? Stop, "be still and know that I am God." If you have never had a spiritual knowing from the Holy Spirit, then don't try to get it by acting like it happened. Pastor James Robinson, of whom I deeply respect, said years ago one night, in one of his crusades, "A broken man knows a broken man." When the Holy Spirit breaks you from Vainglory, Pride, Insensitivity, and many evils we are to talk about later, you will know people He has broken as they enter into your life through God's willingness and purpose. These men, women, and children will be and are broken before God and man. It is an absolute. From this breaking you will receive spiritual peace. It is a virtue, a gift, a spiritual feeling you cannot and will not ever describe, only given by the Holy Spirit to those who ask and are determined to discipline themselves to the obedience of God's statues, His judgments and commandments.

Have you ever seen a horse out at pasture? You watch and give notice to a horse that is not yet broken to ride and is not workable. That horse will run around the pastures kicking and acting up. His tail in the air, his ears up, his mane flowing in the wind as he sprints from one place to another. He is high-spirited and unruly, he will not load into a horse trailer to move him from place to place, and once he is in the trailer, after much name-calling, you can't get him unloaded without a struggle. High-spirited and unruly. Now take the same horse, break him to ride and work him under a disciplined master, and now this same animal will become a true, dedicated, loyal, and above all, a usable, productive part of the master or owner's life. There is a great difference in breaking the human spirit and crushing it.

Why is it so hard to see? Why do we fight this simple spiritual application. In the conforming of our life in the world, trying so hard to make it better, yet failure after failure continues and we become so disgusted. The world has an answer for you and me; the world says, "Now this pill will do this and this pill will do that." "Put your patch on and you won't smoke anymore." Remember addiction, the demon, do we pray against him? Of course not, why? Because we know not of this ability to cleanse ourselves spiritually. Find

Scriptures in the Bible, your Bible, get your marking pen out and start marking, highlighting, find those Scriptures you want to work with. Start simple, just a few, and don't overload yourself. No matter what happens, and it will, whatever activity this desire generates, you stand on those Scriptures. It's because of our spiritual ignorance that our spirit has been held in the darkness for so long only to break free because of faith and perseverance. Don't give up!

In those times when I would test the spirit, my spirit, against those that deceived me all my life, I could see failure coming, and sure enough I would fall. Get back up, stand on that Scripture, fall, get back up. I told Satan, "I have given you forty-nine years of my life, now I'm going to give Christ forty-nine years and let's see who the liar is." Be committed. The bumper sticker on the back of a school bus reads, "Get Radical, Serve God." That school bus driver sent a clear but simple message. It took me a very short time to know who the liar was and is, and it didn't take very long to find out I was getting radical. This is one of the lesser reasons I am writing this journal, owe Satan; I owe him for the destruction he caused in my life. Don't let him destroy you and your life. You can retaliate, go spiritual. Serve God the Father, serve God the Son, serve God the Holy Spirit, serve the Trinity.

As the animal needs discipline and training to bring its spirit under control, so it is with our human nature, to bring our nature under control our spirit needs the authority to command that our nature obeys us, you and I, our word is final, not the word of the demon. Your nature should no longer run unruly across the expanse of your life, your tail, and mane in the air, acting like some runaway unbridled animal. In John 16:33, Christ, in His last words, said, "Take courage I have overcome the world." What He says here is for us to be strong, have courage to continue on in this battle because He is the ultimate power spiritually. To overcome means to get the better of your competition. You struggle, you conquer to master over, overpower, or overwhelm. Using the name of Jesus Christ, every demon's knee has to bend; he has to leave, sooner or later.

As long as you and I have faith, a will to persevere and not give up and cave in to our old self, we can with divine energy, God's grace, move forward to engage and rebuke the devil's demonic energy that unknowingly we have lived with and have succumbed to. By our own spiritual ignorance we become the image of those who destroy our life. By our spiritual wisdom through Christ and the Holy Spirit, we can change and become the image of their righteousness. Becoming who we really are and were meant to be.

One last word on the devil Insensibility, he will deaden your soul then brings death to the mind, and after that he brings death of the body. Be careful, if you are in denial, it's never your fault. You deny the truth, you deny reality, and you cannot accept the fact you are wrong at times, and for sure won't admit it. You have got a problem with you know who! When you eradicate Self-love, Vainglory and Insensibility all the things that derive from them are eradicated as well. That is why humbleness is so strong. Once you rebuke Self-love out of your house, it leaves a vacant space. Remember? When you kick that spirit out, you have the place swept clean. Well, now you must be ready to fill that place with the Lord's Spirit, His virtues, the devotion to God in faith, these are the marks of true love. Love needs your vacant space to live in. We must unite ourselves to God and each other, and when this happens, this account contains the unchanging permanence of all blessings. What I mean is that all blessings become permanent. The Holy Spirit cannot be moved by the weaker demonic spirit of any kind, no matter who he tells you he is or how loud his lying screams are. Tell him or it, "I rebuke you, in the name of Jesus Christ." When you and I travel down this narrow path together, we will be purified over a period of time. Christ wants to bring us before God the Father without stain or blemish. We must make ourselves the devil's enemy. I have become the enemy of the one that stole all of those years of my past life.

In our many days alone within ourselves, we continue to feel empty. And we are alone if we continue to live a worldly life. Alone inside, no one understands the love some of us have for the things too corruptible, evil, even some so corruptible the sensuous inner joy to kill another person or persons God made. He created every man, woman, and child, and along comes this insensitive possessed person who will destroy them for his own lusting carnal self. But at the same time this devil-driving spirit is killing the life of the person who has given him shelter and warmth, 24-7, every day, every night, and depending on how many are in your house and how much demonic energy they can promote will foretell your actions at any given time. Does this sound repetitious? I hope so. Can we make our picture clearer? Can we paint a more pronounced, larger than life, spiritual picture for you to see before you get the message? You and I, we, all of us, live under a spiritual umbrella. Stop and think, this umbrella is over you. You and I, we, cannot exist without our spirit within us. Remember at the beginning, body or flesh, soul and spirit. Three properties that make our human nature function as a person.

Under the devil's umbrella our spiritual energy is supplied to the flesh by way of spiritual dominating unclean beings. We, through spiritual ignorance, have an alliance with these energy sources. Each one depending on its position in the Satanic realm as to how strong it is and how much or how little energy it can use to propel our flesh in the direction they want it to travel, we in turn call these movements passions. Under the canopy of this umbrella, I am bound to do the fleshly sinful, and sometimes evil desires. My soul all of this time is in an evil state. Unwilling to fight against this unclean energy. The soul, yours and mine, all of us at this time is in bondage to the horde of its savage masters. My spirit is kept in the dark, bound and tied within the suffering soul. Looking through the spiritual door we have opened wide for you, how can you not see the heinous inter-workings that cause for some of us the corruption and suffering in our life? Whatever you do, whatever you do, whatever you do, do not read this book, these writings, and say I am not included, I am not a sinner, I am a good person, these things are not part of me and my life. If you cannot remember when you have struck out at your neighbor verbally, when you have cursed the person in your family. When you—now listen to this one and tell me you are not controlled by an insensitive spirit—when you try to control everything in your family and every family of your children, your grandchildren, and your friend's families included. Your word is always the best advice. Your vision on how they should live and act is always the unapproachable unforgiving word of law. You have all of the answers to every situation that arises. You think inside yourself how clever I am, they all think I am so great. They better do as I say, or I'll make them pay one way or the other. Some men, but mostly women, have this spirit of insensibility that tries to dominate all movements in their men and children at older ages; they do not want to lose that authority figure. You push your husbands into a form of existence only. The men lose all respect. You know more than your stupid husband, you are so clever and smart, you can see through him and everything he does. If he ever does anything right, it's because you told him to. If he rebels and wants to be his own person, you, the clever one, humiliate him in front of others, and over a period of time he will never make a decision; he never voices his opinion. And as years pass, you with your self-love (Vainglory), your hard heart and sharp tongue (insensibility) will pay tribute to the form of evil that has possessed you. Your pride will be crushed because the family no longer listens to your continuous verbalization, because your talking will become incessant. You will hear these words, "Mother! Will you please shut up, just shut up and stop talking. You're driving us all crazy." And as I watch these poor women who have striven for years to achieve their high calling, as the spirit of self-love and pride continually blind them from the reality of life around them, I wonder why, why do these people, men and women, ignore the tribulation that slowly comes upon them. Why can't you see what you are doing to your loved ones. Your family, your neighbor, who is known and unknown. Men, don't get self-righteous. Many of you are held by and controlled by this demon.

Our prayer for all of those that are consumed with the evil energies of their human sin nature and their unquestionable ignorance of God and His divine energies is "forgive them, for they know not what they do." In Luke chapter 23, verse 34, Christ, as He hangs from the cross, asks God the Father to forgive those that kill Him, because it is actually not their fault but the evil energies that possess them and propel them and their thinking. Their mind, like ours, at times, mine included, draws a blank, a misuse of our own powers. With our insensitive power, we unknowingly divorce our nature from God's will and continue on that perverted road. St. Maximos the Confessor, a spiritual saint of the Church in the sixth century, writes, "The devil has deceived us by his guile, in a malicious and cunning way. He, the devil, has perverted the truth and in this manner has divided humanity, cutting it up into opinions and fantasies." How many times do our friends, especially politicians, pervert the truth? I no longer can stand the verbalization "well, in my opinion," "who cares!"

Yours and mine, our opinions are of two properties. One, it must be the truth, to be able to be consumed into the divine energy of God, that propels you and I in our life's struggle, but with love and peace. Two, it will be the perverted or fractured truth or outright lie that St. Maximos talks about, and that is consumed by my demon, for as I lie to you or deny the truth and verbalize you with my great intellectual knowledge I'm feeding the very one that blinds me from the actual truth. This is an absolute! There is no other way.

Is it easier to look through this open door, you and me, and see an invisible fence approaching? Standing in the doorway and looking down across the tops of the fence posts that now proceed out from us past the horizon. And as the first anchor post approaches, it now separates the open door into two sides, right or left, now, no walking down the center and trying to straddle the fence, one foot in the world, one foot in the church. You make the decision. I'm going to the left, stay in my same old life my worldly life, or step to the right and enter into a new life with Christ, His Father God and the Holy Spirit, the God of our spiritual fulfillment, who unites us with all spiritual activity that is righteous before God, helping us become more and more the image of our Father God, our Creator and Lord.

You are now under the umbrella of divine grace. Or choose number two and go to the left side of the fence, stay in your same old rut, and be under the spiritual umbrella of the darkness and its demons.

Chapter 12
Death

It is time that we look at this mystery. Who is he? Where did he come from? Why do we fear this wretched spirit, and do we have to fear him as he comes into our life?

Many questions regarding death, with very few answers to give.

As we try to find a solution to the fear problem, we must try to find a beginning. In trying to research the spiritual path that death walks, we must, without fear, try to walk through his history. Looking for the signs and the writing of those who were able, by God's Grace, His divine energy, to show us in depth what actually take place when this spirit moves or acts.

We must now step inside the doorway and, protected by God's grace, we ask that our Lord open our mind, give us the spiritual eyes we need to see the state of this particular property or nature, the image of death, and who he is. Are you listening to this silence? It's time to pay attention. Silence makes you virtuous, just as fasting makes you more spiritual. Quit eating if you have your chips and Coke nearby.

With this session you, and only you, can decide what your final outlook can be. Death brings different departures and makes us believe, he, Death, and only Death, has the last word. Nonsense! God has the last word! You and I have next to the last word. Don't you ever forget it, because I will not, even if you do. You make this stony, hard, and darkened spirit your servant by your discipline, by your spiritual knowledge of him, and your obedience to follow the narrow path. Your conception of death after this session, hopefully, will change as did mine. Be in constant vigil, meditate on what you read and hear.

Is Death's voice that of a raging and raving creature as is some of the other we have identified? Or is he the silent persuader bringing to us the despondency and distress of leaving before we have even left?

Sometimes, when death occurs in our families and our loved ones leave, we detach ourselves from him as soon as possible. Death is not something we Christians, Gentiles, Pagans, or Atheists think much about. But, since we are looking into and are in it, let's not deny Death's presence in our lives. If you want to change your life, you and I must, in truth, look at these different aspects. What we identify as natural feelings are sometimes demonic spiritual powers trying to establish, or have established, sinful habits. The unclean spirit says, "Oh! That's just natural and everybody does it." No, everybody does not do it. Lord, have mercy.

There are old saints, men of God, men who lived for God throughout the centuries who lived and died as their time came. They wrote about death and their disciples wrote for them. This information comes from men in the fourth and fifth centuries up to the seventeenth and eighteenth centuries. These writings have of late been brought to us because someone has translated these writings into English. I will try as I may to leave with you an insight on this subject. I am not declaring; I am not suggesting to you in any way that this subject matter contains is proven physically or is of any such notion. But we must, as human beings created in God's image, be able to behold the evil and holy spiritual powers. Make our choice on and by our own willingness, our free choice to follow the wide road that leads to death, or follow the narrow path leading to life.

Take your Bible, open to the Book of Matthew chapter 7, verse 13 and 14.

> "Enter by the narrow gate; for the gate is wide and the way is easy that leads to destruction, and those who enter by it are many. For the gate is narrow and the way is hard that leads to life and those who find it are few." Christ said, "Enter by the narrow gate."

These are the words of your creator, he who created you and me, the very One who is spiritually divine and sinless as a natural man. What gate is narrow? If the gate spiritually is narrow, it means, spiritually, not many will pass through. Not that it will not allow it, but because the way is hard, not many care to enter. The path is hard and narrow in its climb, winding through our sufferings, our toils, and disappointments. But, the Lord said, "This path leads to life," the final ecstasy, our victory over death.

Lord Jesus Christ, Son of God, have mercy on me, a sinner.

For the gate is wide and the way is easy, this road leads to destruction. Death awaits at this end. This road is a highway for the world and man it's so easy to party down. Live today. Tomorrow may not come. It is truly astonishing how when we are so insecure, that we make excuses for our behavior by including Death. "It's his fault. I want to enjoy all of this around me. I want to go and see all of the paces I've heard about, eat food, lots of booze, lots of women. We can go and crash and start over in the morning. Have you got a joint? I'm out. We gotta have fun, man. We could die and look what we would have missed!" On and on and on.

Death smiles. He knows it's only a matter of time, of which he has plenty. Stay on the wide road. Physical and spiritual death which, through your life, has already started at birth and will continue. Remember Death's time clock was punched when you were born. Don't get too lost in your ego and pride. What is your answer when you start shedding hot tears? Sudden death will not come. You and your soul will pay the high price with a slow and agonizing life in later years.

The Book of John chapter 21, verse 18 states, "Truly, truly, I say to you, when you were young, you girded yourself and walked where you would; but when you are old you will stretch out your hands and another will gird you and carry you where you do not wish to go." When the Lord spoke these words and he said, "Truly, truly," you can take this to the bank. It is an absolute. This is coming from divine grace himself, meaning this is the truth—the real truth.

Christ said, "You can when you're young dress yourself and go wherever you please." But, he said, *but* when you are old you will stretch out your hands, meaning you surrender to your captors and they who you wined and dined with (all of those evils ones) now become your master and they will carry you where you do not want to go. And, if I read this correctly, it also means you no longer dress yourself. They will dress you as they see fitting for their occasion. So, since this is not physical but a spiritual lesson, you tell me who's coming and who is going and who is in control of your life when you lose your youth; your hair starts to turn gray, and your skin wrinkles. Remember in our writings we said as we get older and weaker, they get stronger and acquire from us that of an obedient servant attitude and now in cowardly fear we are led by the demons into the darkness. By dressing us for their occasions, they can send you and me into any type of circumstance and we will do their work for them.

This is a sickness, a spiritual sickness, that your soul has acquired over years of transgressions brought on by you and only you.

Spiritually we have two free choices: one is life, one is death.

One is light, the other darkness.

One is wisdom, the other ignorance.

One is to obey, the other disobedience.

One is love, the other hate.

And many more for those that make their own free choice, or by their own free will choose death or life.

Satan lies to us when we look from our worldly position toward a spiritual change of any kind unless it's more demeaning than our life already is. He still lies to us because he will tell us how smart we are to make this decision, all along watching us fall lower and lower as our life passes by.

The Book of Ezekiel, Old Testament, chapter 36, verses 26 and 27 writes, "God said, 'Moreover I will give you a new heart and put a new spirit within you and I will remove the heart of stone from your flesh and give you a heart of flesh. And I will put my spirit within you and cause you to walk in my statutes and you will be careful to observe my ordinances.'"

Now, how much difference can you see here? Satan, who hides in the darkness of our souls, will not tell us what's going on in our spiritual life. He, Satan, continues to pull us by sensuous feelings in the opposite direction, away from our original purpose in life, which was to have a relationship with God our Creator. Satan wants to drag me as a prisoner down into Hades with him and his filthy buddies, while the Lord is saying, "If you choose me I will take out that heart of stone." We both know that means insensitivity and self-love with pride and ignorance, and our spirit is renewed and it starts to control the flesh. And a soft heart is given us. So that the change is going to be more easy, the Lord gives us his Spirit, the Holy One, and with the Holy Spirit guiding our spirit, we can gain the wisdom to follow spiritual laws and statues that will prohibit our soul from digesting and regurgitating the unclean iniquities and waste from our prior life.

Which promise do you want? Which promise did I take? I choose life.

I gave Satan all of those years. Now I'm giving Christ His years. I'm not guessing who the liar is. I know today, as I did back a number of years ago, Christ has saved my life. By his truth in showing us which spirit works, we can, by free choice, live in now and after death. We will still have a life forever and ever.

Webster's New World College Dictionary explains death as an end to a struggle, a permanent ending. If we are true Christians and believe Christ as to what He speaks is absolute truth, then what Christ speaks through his pastors, his priests, and his people, then it is truly the end of our worldly struggle and an end to our pain and suffering—a permanent end to both pain and suffering, but not a permanent end to your spiritual life as some would have us believe.

For our reference we look to *Life after Death* by Metropolitan Nafpaklos Hierotheos, translated by Esther Williams. He writes, "To be convinced of the existence of the other life as a matter of inner spiritual sensitivity. For even if someone should rise from the dead it could be misconstrued as fantasy."

Why is it that no one looks at death as a fantasy? We all look at him as an absolute. The world says, "Death and taxes," right? The world says death is "lights out." "It's over, put 'em in the ground." After a number of years, the generations pass by the grave and lost is that person's identity. A reminder of the permanence of death and seen as an absolute, fear comes with death to our minds and our souls. We, because of our ignorance, accept both of these feelings as truth and succumb to the world and its thinking. Fear of death now comes.

Now, since when are we going to lie as the world tell us, "It's over"? Do they know anything spiritual? No! If it cannot be proven by "seeing" or "reasoning" or "science," then it is not proven useful and unbelievers say so. You know the feeling.

This is why you and I cannot change our inner selves' position of authority to "be able to be me."

Because you can't see it being done, because reasoning does help, because science gives us one more pill and for sure it doesn't help (it compounds the problems sometimes). Again I'm not saying medication is not a great thing, because it is. I take it myself. But let's be truthful. I can take a pill to cleanse my kidneys, but I haven't found one yet that will clean my soul. When it comes to cleaning up that mess, I have to go spiritual. I have to find the spirit who can go in there and start with authority, command with authority, evict with authority; because I am asking Him to clean out an idolatrous surrounding, a place of evil, a place that has influenced my body to act and perform as an addicted being (addicted not to one idol but many).

My body groans again and again. My flesh wants to reject the influence of the spirit who has come through prayer to save me from death and my thinking of that death. Then in those days, "Absolute destruction." The voices come and go. The voices change in pitch and tone. They hate my determination to be me. They hate my obedience to the Bible scriptures. The voice of my brain and in my brain scream at my prayer time and disrupt my days and weeks and months with their conduct, lying and promising, fantasizing, horrid dreams and such dishonorable things. They will pass.

Before I was a Christian, I had a vision of a demon one night. He came to give me a message from Satan, of whom I had honored in previous times. He said if I continued down this path, Death was waiting for me at the end of this tunnel I was sliding down. I was in a free fall, screaming as I began to enter the darkness below. I awoke. I had a pistol under my pillow. You know, we all sleep with a pistol under our pillows, right? In those days I was extremely fearful, and because I didn't want certain things to happen to me, in my limited reasoning, I was protecting myself. I tried to shoot the demon and in the end, almost shot my friend who had given me a place to stay, in his home, and so as you would expect, he asked me to leave. I did.

But back to this present day, it's the now we are talking about. No matter what the voice or voices in you are saying, you must go to Christ to receive your spiritual eyes and see this spirit as he truly is. Death is not who you and I have been told he is. He, Death, does not have a hold on me or you. He does not bring a permanent ending to our life. There will be a life after we leave here. He, Death, cannot stop me from moving across to the other side. You must believe who is good, strong, loving, and compassionate. You must believe the movement of the Holy Spirit in you will conquer all things, visible and invisible, known and unknown, no matter who is evil. This is an absolute. Stand on this with your total self, with faith as your foundation, salvation as your goal. Try to understand the depth of his scriptures. Death hates this truth because it makes him out a liar.

In your Bible, Luke chapter 16, verse 17, Christ is speaking. He is speaking to the Pharisees, to the most religious people in the church of that day, but be alert for they, the Pharisees, are still around to this day. Men deny Christ and his teaching today as they have for years and years and as the Pharisees did. "And it is easier for heaven and earth to pass, than one tittle of the law to fail" (Luke 16:17). "Tittle" in Hebrew means a dot, a period or dot. Christ says that at no time will one or any of his spiritual laws fail. Heaven will pass away, Earth will pass away, but his covenant—God's ordinances, statues, and commandments—will not fail. A spiritual absolute! Truth!

You and I can believe with all of our heart and soul and know that not one dot in all of His writings will fail us. Those of us that believe will never see death. Life is an absolute because His law has said so. This belief is called faith.

Glory be to the Father, Son, and the Holy Spirit.

From the *Revell Bible Dictionary*, the term death is explained in two parts:

1. The end of a biological life
2. The moral and spiritual state of human beings separated from God

Let us look now to the Holy Bible and try without great verbalization, to try in a simple way to see death in a different light. The Old Testament, Isaiah chapter 6, verse 6 states, "Also the sons of the stranger, that join themselves to the Lord, to serve Him and to love the name of the Lord, to be His servants, every one that keep my Sabbath from polluting it, and taketh hold of my covenant."

So any man, woman, or child is welcome. So I'm not the song of a stranger to God, but yet if I keep His spiritual laws, I will be welcome in His kingdom.

But for those of us who refuse to accept the way of the narrow path, he explains it this way: "Yea they are greedy dogs which can never have enough, and they are shepherds that cannot understand, they all look to their own way, every one for his own gain" (Isa. 56:11).

Have you seen this person lately? Of course you have. I know one quite well. In fact, I know him really well. It's me he's talking about, the old me, the stranger that was before who I am now. But my spiritual conversion has let me understand and now I can see. No longer am I the "dumb dog that cannot bark, always sleeping, lying down, loving to slumber."; by the way, this is verse 10, in case you didn't see it.

What does this have to do with death? Read on to chapter 57, verses 1–2.

> The righteous perisheth, and no man layeth it to heart: and merciful men are taken away, none considering that the righteous is taken away from the evil to come. He shall enter into peace; they shall rest in their beds, each one walking in their uprightness.

We all mourn for our close friends and relations that pass away, some more than others. The Lord said, "Blessed are they that mourn, for they shall be comforted." But look now into the world of the Holy Spirit and see the unseeable by reading spiritual writings. These people were taken up into His kingdom. They were righteous, they are with him, Isaiah says. Let it be in your heart. Don't be one that mourns for years and is mad at God for taking your favorite person. That person is with his or her Creator. They are at peace finally. Their soul is with God and their body at rest, each and every one. No one is left out, no exceptions. All of the sons and daughters of the stranger will be accepted because they kept his covenant. Death is not the end for the believer but the door to an endless life beyond the seeable.

Death is not a natural occurrence. Death comes from the fall of Adam. Of those things Satan gave us. Something he hides from us is the true explanation of what the spirit of death actually is. If we want to believe the light, the word, the Christ. If not, believe the darkness and stay blind, and maybe because Satan is such a nice guy, you will end up as the dog that can't bark, that sleeps his life away. Never able to understand, probably because you like it so!

Now our biological life ends and here we go, looking into the space called the hereafter, our soul very much alive. We are following the narrow path. I will not take the wide road as the world sees it. The narrow path is the way of the church, the spiritual path. The narrow path leads to life, and to receive life, you and I must go together, walk into and explore the other side; using the narrow path may be more difficult but surely much safer. Let us leave death now and look at our soul. So as the body passes into its lifeless form when death occurs, the soul separates from the body and now the soul must cross over into the other side, the other world. Remember when we talked about being still.

> And Moses said unto them "stand still and I will hear what the Lord will command concerning you." (Num. 9:8)

Be still and know that I am God. (Ps. 46:10)

When we talk about where your soul and my soul are going, you should be still and contemplate your soul's journey before the trip time actually becomes a reality. I have spent hours trying to just get started with an explanation of something that for some like me it took years to acquire.

To explain the breakdown between the body, our flesh, the soul or heart, as sometimes it is called, and our spirit, because of repetition, please be fair, and enlightened with the ability to see that which I can only do with your help.

1. The body or flesh

    The outer shell, our physical self, our fleshly, worldly self, controlled by our sin nature and that which we call normal in our life and times. We all are familiar with this part of our makeup.

2. The soul

    The inner self, not ever me, is familiar with this part of our makeup, so we must, to be open, try to explain in simplicity who she is. She is who you are, not your mind, not your spirit, but who you really are. She is alive and is attached to our inner self by being tied to the body at birth and will separate from the body at the time of death. She is called our soul. When death happens, this beautiful part of who you are goes into the supernatural. God creates the soul for each created body, and the soul knows God, even though the body she loves might deny her that choice.

3. The spirit

    Our spirit, placed in with the soul at the time of our birth, our spirit connects with the spiritual realm and conveys with the soul what it sees and hears from that realm to the body the soul and spirit are in union.

I was still under the control of the spirit of addiction when my soul started screaming in fear of where it might be sent. In the book *After Death* by Father Vasilios Bakogiannis, the question is asked, "How can people seek to understand eternal life when they are unable to comprehend the very world they live in they cannot understand what it sees and hears from that relationship the visible? So how can they understand the invisible?"

So to try to make sense out of this; we, you and I, must see it in its simplicity. Truth lays firm and sound in its house, surrounded and guided by simplicity and humbleness. Let me be clear! In great humility I come before you. Not in pride, not in vainglory, not in anything material or of this world. I write only to those that want change or are looking to go deeper in their spiritual awareness. There was a man on television, a commentator, describing an Olympic athlete that was to perform during the games. And the commentator says to his fellow associate, "Well, (this person) is so dumb that (this person) cannot put two paragraphs together, but is certainly a fine athlete," and so could I be the one included in the description, "too dumb to put two paragraphs together." My wife and I laugh sometimes because I continually am asking her how to spell certain words.

Lord, have mercy on my soul.

But, because of the spiritual beauty, the peace that only understanding can bring, we now open by God's grace, his divine energy, the door to the world that awaits those of us who with open mind want the truth about the spirit world. This particular explanation comes from the book *The Ascetical Homilies of Saint Isaac the Syrian* translated by the Holy Transfiguration Monastery, Boston Massachusetts.

Because in previous chapters and paragraphs I have mentioned the world, society, the flesh, and the darkness, which leads us through or by our sinful nature into a self-destructive lifestyle, I need to explain. We talked about the body, soul, and spirit and how can we change by becoming more spiritual and less fleshly or worldly. Now we will look at the soul and spirit. So to understand this transition, let us look at the knowledge. Then after knowledge we will look at faith. Knowledge and faith work against each other. Knowledge by itself cannot, will not ever reach the high that faith brings to the soul and set the spirit free.

Now, look at the knowledge as a property. Hold knowledge in your left hand, arms outstretched, palms up, and there sits knowledge in the left hand. Do the same with faith, but now put faith in your right hand. Both are properties, both are unseeable, but yet we must look at them in such a way that we can understand their presence in our inner self. To see knowledge as he is, we must open our spiritual door wide enough to see why our soul is affected by the wall that knowledge builds.

We must depend now on our spirit to convey to us the ability to see what the "eye has not seen and the ear has not heard." Most of us have only used our fleshly self to try to understand our life. Now we can use our spirit for the first time as our soul tries to break out of the prison she has been in all of these years. So we acquire knowledge through investigation through examination, through reading of others, proof of groundwork, within the realm of material or seeable things. Knowledge has boundaries that cannot go beyond what the eye can actually see. Nature is itself as far as knowledge can go. Take water for instance, man cannot walk on water because knowledge will say that water cannot support upon its back the footsteps of the body. Fire burns the man who gets too close to it, and our knowledge protects us with the fear of opposing anything beyond nature because it will bring us into peril.

So as knowledge uses natures as its boundaries, it limits itself to the natural world. Knowledge wants to cleave to the love of the body; he wants to gather up provisions: wealth, vainglory (honor), adornment, rest for the body. Meaning: we want to keep our body rested, no adversity, no stress, guarding our nature from anything that would there by cause us harm. Knowledge wants constant personal attention to rational wisdom. (This is worldly, being wise because you can find reasoning or a reason for whatever you are doing.) Knowledge really gushes out with such novelties, such as inventions, the arts, science doctrines, knowledge to be suitable to be in high places of governing.

Knowledge is dominated by the body, and the body introduces to the mind its total concern for the world and nothing else. This knowledge is common, rude, and boorish; it does not reckon that there is soulish power or spiritual power. It does not believe that there is any kind of driving power. It takes into *no* account that God is the hidden steersman over man. Knowledge keeps the soul and spirit in a prison of darkness and despair. His knowledge says to the mind that there is no divine governing over any invisible thing. Yet knowledge is in continual fear with the body and is prey to those that create faint-heartedness, sorrow, despair, fear of demons, rumors of thieves, reports of murder, anxiety over illness, concern over lack or wants of necessities, fear of death, fear of suffering, fear of wild beasts, and all such things.

St. Isaac says, "Knowledge is a sea made turbulent by great waves at every hour of the night and day." Knowledge with all its worldly greatness does not know how to cast its care upon God through the confidence and trust that faith in Christ brings us. It tells the body, we are all alone in this world, just you and me, and without me, your knowledge, you are nothing. But knowledge can investigate the small faults of other men and women and what might cause those faults and weaknesses, and this aids him to cunningly employ devices and crafty ways to dishonor that man or woman and as these aids the world more and more through our life we fall for Pride's voice calling us to our destruction. You know, pride, the one that attributes every good thing to itself, and does *not* ever refer it to God. Among the properties of knowledge is that this knowledge belongs to those oppose faith. This is as St. Isaac stated, "shallow knowledge," for it is naked of all concern for God.

All knowledge is a gift from God at our birth. It is bestowed by God on the nature of rational beings at their creation. It is simple and undivided by according to its activity knowledge will undergo changes and divisions according to a man's diligence and his methods (St. Isaac, homily fifty-two).

Remember the tree of good and evil (Gen. 2:9). The tree that uproots love is implanted in this very knowledge. Avarice, the demon, lover of material things, and Pride, with Vainglory, lovers of self, and any other demon, unclean spirit, or beings form the darkness uses knowledge as a path or roadway. It is a means of travel for them because our soul and spirit are prisoners, voiceless and cold, unable to motivate the righteous body as it succumbs to passion after passion in our lifetime. They, the soul and the spirit, are the body's lifeline, and because unbelief is so strong they remain powerless to knowledge.

Faith, on the other hand, is simplicity. Read Colossians chapter 3, verse 22, "Come as servants with simple hearts and glorify God." Read Matthew chapter 18, verses 3–4, Christ is speaking, "Verily I say unto you, except you be converted and become as little children, you shall not enter into the kingdom of heaven. Whosoever shall humble Himself as this little child, the same is greatest in the kingdom of heaven."

Faith comes with diving assistance, it enters into our soul, which has surrendered herself to God, and because of His help, she, our soul, will never think of herself as being bound by knowledge. She, the soul, will be in awestruck wonder, being still, being silent, being able to feel God's providence, His presence, which will cleave to her and never leave her, no matter where she might go.

Read Matthew chapter 21, verse 21. Christ is speaking, "Truly I say to you, if you have faith, and do not doubt, you shall not only do what was done to the fig tree, but even if you say to this mountain 'Be taken up and cast into the sea,' it shall happen." Faith brings God's immeasurable love. You cannot measure his love because it is so deep it has no bottom or boundaries. God's power and might, which becomes ours as our faith gets stronger, is greater than anything we might ask, think, or conceive.

Faith in God's grace, giving you and me His divine energy, will not let us tolerate any deliberations, reasoning, investigating, proving by eyesight the things beyond our ability to see. Faith is higher than nature, faith looks to the supernatural, the seen and unseen, those things heard and unheard.

Faith is pure and simple and it is single. Meaning one and only one of its kind. Faith knows the impossible can be acquired and lights up the soul and spirit with a diving light that illumines and glows with the love of God and the Holy Spirit. Demons can see the soul of this person shining a light as bright as the sun. Christ carries this diving light in his human nature as we have explained in his divine nature also. So in our conversion from a person of intellect and knowledge, worldly and fleshly we become Christlike and start to receive His gifts. Faith being one of those gifts and the soul takes on his illumination. Faith has no fear; faith is not ruled by fear or pride, vainglory, love of self-money, or any of the things that the darkness hides in. An unbeliever has all of this baggage hanging around all through his life because knowledge is fed by the things unseen; while it is exhausting, it is self-proving and disproving in its journey to be wise and show great wisdom, but yet bound to the world, its primary aim is to oppose faith and prove to all around that knowledge is far higher and greater than faith, yet all the while it is being ruled by the very ones it cannot see. And the darkness loves it so. Trying to prove the unseen doesn't exist but engulfed in it and by it.

Faith not held by any boundaries things of nature or the supernatural. Read Mark 16 verse 17; Christ speaks, "And these signs will accompany those who have believed in my name, they will cast out demons. They will pick up serpents, or if they happen to drink any deadly poison, it shall not hurt them: they will lay their hands on the sick and they, the sick, will recover." Both the things of nature and the supernatural will be at the will of those who have faith and believe. Remember when Peter stepped out of the boat, walked on the water toward Christ, but then began to sink, fear took hold of his feet and started to pull him towards the deep (Matt. 14:29–32). Christ reached out and pulled him up and said to Peter, "O you of little faith. Why did you doubt?" But when we read the next verse—and this verse is almost always left out of the sermons, verse 32—and when they got into the boat, the wind stopped.

How many times in our conversion period does the wind blow, big waves come, and after we continue and win our battle with the spirit of unbelief and doubt we find Christ is there to pull us free from their grasp and the wind stops blowing and the waves diminish and disappear and our peace returns?

In chapter 11, verse 5 in the Book of Ecclesiastes, it says, "As you do not know the way of the spirit, no how the bones grow in the womb of her that is with child. Even so, you knowest not the works of God, he makes all things." The reason I ask you to read this scripture is that in your own world, our inside of us world, we without the spirit of God, the Holy Spirit, cannot and will never know how he works in our inner and outer life, to give us peace and wisdom, wisdom to get past the boundaries of knowledge, the set boundaries of the world, and above all deliver us from the boundaries set for us by the unclean ones that have ruled our past life and without Christ our future life. Then the Lord God formed man of dust from the ground, and breathed into his nostrils the breath of life; and man became a living soul. According to Genesis chapter 2, verse 7, the soul and the spirit take on life by the very breath of God at that time and so today, this has or will take the place of His breath, His presence in our life. When he calls your soul your life ends. Period. An absolute.

The description of the heart of a person is the person's soul. It is unseeable but, because we cannot see it doesn't mean it is not present in our everyday life. Like in our previous writings, we said Satan is after your soul. He could care less about your body once the soul leaves. So even the unbeliever who claims nothing of Lord's presence can be found in him, his denial, his anger, his fear, his determination, he still has and will always have an open door in his life. Christ can enter in anytime He feels free to do so and the unbeliever has absolutely no control. Christ can, will, and does have control over the soul of every human being ever born on this Earth. From Adam's soul to yours and mine, will your soul, filled full of unbelief, stand before Christ?

> So also it is written "the first man Adam became a living soul." the Last Adam [Christ] became a life giving spirit [our spirit to His spirit]. However the spiritual is not first, but the natural is first. Then comes the spiritual. [First we are natural. Later we can become spiritual] and just as we have been born in the image of the earthly [natural] we shall also bear the image of the heavenly. (1 Cor. 15:45–49)

AM I THE ONE YOU ARE LOOKING FOR?

You cannot escape. You can run, in all of your great knowledge, run, shake your fist, grit your teeth, demanding the ground to open up and swallow you before you would go to Christ. Take your money, buy whatever, wherever, whenever, but he still has control. You are born of His image. You have a soul. He and only He gives out of His love for you, and a spirit made in his image so God can contact you any time in your life, dead or alive, because your soul never dies, and both your soul and God shall live forever. But it is the environment that the soul lives in, that is the unavoidable question. You can deny it, but you cannot change anything by your denial.

Your soul, who you are, the feeling of self, and your love for whoever or wherever and all of whoever you will be here on Earth and wherever you might be at that time, your soul belongs to Him—Christ. He has first choice as to the environment you will live in, because you are your soul.

In 2 John chapter 5, verses 21–22, Christ is speaking to the Jews who were seeking to kill him (verse 18). "For just as the Father raises the dead and gives them life, even so the son also gives life to who he wishes" (He, Christ, has the authority to give you life or death, as he wishes), "For not even the Father [God] judges anyone, but He has given all judgment to the son." Christ is the final judge on Earth. You and I can run and soak up all the pleasures we can find, keep our sounds drowning in our cesspool of sinfulness and life of the flesh. Even if you are one of those that states, "Who? Me? I'm not a sinner!" Yup, you too. Your soul is going to be right there beside the druggies and alcoholics and the addicted.

The soulish part of our self is the separator, because the spirit, our spirit, is part of our soul and the two live in our body, for easier or simpler clarification.

> And he [(Elijah] stretched himself up the child three times and cried unto the Lord and said, "'I pray thee, let this child's soul come into him again." And the Lord heard the voice of Elijah and the soul of the child came into him again, and he revived. (1 Kings 17:21–22)

The child died. His soul separated from his body and the prayer goes up to the Creator. Please send the soul back into the child so he can live, and it was done, because God willed it. Your soul and my soul are living property. Because of our ignorance and because we can't see it does not mean it doesn't exist.

"As the Lord liveth and as thy soul liveth, I will not leave thee" (2 Kings 2:2).

This man is making a commitment to the Lord and to the other man. He says, "As long as your soul is alive I will not leave you." "Though I were perfect yet would not know my own soul. I would despise my life" (Job 9:21). What Job is talking about is without God, even if Job was perfect, he would not know his own soul and therefore he would live his life in contempt and scorn—to dislike his own life.

Even if you have knowledge and money, even if you don't have money or knowledge, it makes no difference at all. You still do not know your own soul. You cannot know who you really are even if you think you are perfect. The person has to know the soul before the life of that person can live in peace and harmony, and the only way is through the spirit. This is why the person must become "spiritual."

We cannot become spiritual until we use our spirit to connect to the Lord, and at that time the soul, who is the receiver or container of all things from the Lord, now starts to be filled with divine energy and starts to become illumined (lit up). And, when this happens, "The law of the Lord is perfect, restoring the soul, the testimony of the Lord is sure, making wise the simple" (Ps. 19:7). This verse makes us see that if we follow the Lord's statutes, ordinances, His principles and His ways—which all are spiritual laws—then our soul—which was dead in sin, dark in its interior, and lifeless because of its prison boundaries—can now be restored to its original purpose. To give life to the body, a new life, peace, love, kindness, and in that transition period the soul filled with divine energy overpowers the authority of the habits and those that hide in dark rooms, overpowers the flesh and worldly ways, overpowers the mind and takes knowledge within itself. The man's knowledge is filled with divine energy and comes out of the soul through the spirit as spiritual wisdom.

This is where wisdom comes from not out of your head but out of your soul. "He will make the simple wise." So He restores our soul, and because we have faith and believe He gives us His spiritual wisdom. Now we become spiritual, soulish and spiritual, with spiritual wisdom. Father Seraphim Rose said in his book *Not of this World*, "We must not continue to walk the cross arms of the cross but we must go vertical into Christ." We must take the plunge, and every bad habit in you is going to scream, "Don't do it!" But deep into Christ, you take your soul and your spirit will be with you, and above all else, Christ will be with you.

> To Thee O Lord, I lift up my soul. O, my God in Thee I trust, do not let me be ashamed; do not let my enemy exult over me. Indeed, none of those who wait for thee will be ashamed; but those who deal treacherously will be ashamed. (Ps. 25:1–3)

Because many of us do not have the boldness to speak out at the times, we are confronted by someone who has a different opinion; we hesitate and then become silent. This shameful thing happens in our Christian walk. Sometimes we are ashamed to admit our belief in God, and so the unbeliever or atheist confronts us and makes us feel like a fool. People who believe in a different God than ours confront us with their superior knowledge and power of words, leave us speechless and weak. We become angry with our self for not having the ability and fortitude to speak out and confront their shallow way of thinking.

The Psalmist says, "To Thee O Lord I lift up my soul." The most beautiful part of who you are is your soul. You lift up your soul to God. The Lord cares not about how beautiful your external appearance may be. The Lord looks at the soul and His divine light illumines it when the soul is offered to Him before the time of death.

The man gives the Lord his eternal part, the part or property of the man that lives forever. The soul and the spirit of the man together are eternal properties. They never die. They live forever. The reason man lifts up and gives his soul to God is the simple fact that no one can exult or overpower our God—Father, Son, or Holy Spirit. Once His divine light or energy fills the soul and puts His stamp of ownership on it, no man, no woman, no demon, no unseen or seen being can overpower or take away that which was given to you by your creator. Your soul, you who are now come into being; now you are going to be you.

In conclusion, we know that Death comes when you and I are called by time. Time has its appointed hour for all of us; there is no escape, no excuse. Death rides his black horse into the presence of our being and the soul now separates from the body. Now the soul has no protection. The body lies in the ground and the soul enters into the world of the spirit, the very world you and I have read about and are looking at and into. Without the body to protect it, the soul, you who you are, passes through the doors of mortality into immortality.

Death has completed his world. His job is done. The absolute denial of life forever of the body, full of our sin nature if we walked this Earth without Christ, full of divine nature if we walked with Christ, your choice, my choice, our choice. Death is not a choice if we wait for him to arrive, and as he approaches, his presence being felt in our body, it is too late. Mister Time, which you had plenty of, picks up his suitcase and leaves us. Death and Time work together—one leaves, the other arrives. There are other teachings from men who write from their knowledge and as worldly intellectuals. How do they look at death? In reading Father Seraphim Rose, his book, *The Soul after Death*, he explains the view of those outside of our Christian beliefs. Using Father Seraphim's material, on page 160, Dr. Moody reports, "There is no judgment to come and no hell." On page 161, "The purpose of life on Earth, and of life after death is not the eternal salvation of one's soul, but an unlimited process of growth in 'love' and 'understanding' and 'self-realization.'" On page 160, Dr. Kubler-Ross defines death: "Death is simply a shedding of the physical body, like the butterfly coming out of a cocoon, it is a transition into a higher state of consciousness." In ending this explanation Dr. Kubler-Ross states, "It's like putting away your winter coat when spring comes." The doctor says, "Death is not as unique and final an experience as Christian doctrine has described it, but is a harmless transition into a higher state of consciousness."

Because in all of my years of searching for the truth, again and again, I would, and did, listen to these people, trying to avoid the spiritual traps set for me by the writings of others, and yet I needed to read both sides to get, I thought, a true perspective on the subject. So since Dr. Moody and Dr. Kubler-Ross have given us their opinion on death, now look at what Christ said about death and the soul. This is the parable of the rich man. The rich man said, "And I will say to my soul, 'soul you have many goods laid up for many years to come; take your ease, eat, drink, be merry'" (Luke 12:19). But, God said to him, "You fool! This very night your soul is required of you; and now who will own what you have prepared" (Luke 12:20).

Now we have two different statements from two different perspectives: the world perspective from an intellectual knowledge and the spiritual perspective from the divine creator Himself.

In our next chapter, which is on the soul, some of this information will be used. But, let's take a few minutes to look at what we have just read. The intellectuals in their writings say that at the time of death, "spring is coming. Take off your winter coat. Enjoy! You're going into a higher state of consciousness"—whatever that means. I thought the same thing when I was a drunk. Give me another drink, I want to get higher. I'm not high enough. Give me a joint so I can get higher, on and on and on. Lord, have mercy on my soul.

At the time of death, you're going to shed your cocoon. Your body falls off and now you're just like a beautiful butterfly. Just fly from flower to flower with a care for the past or the future. Just fly around. Where? Where are you in the spring? Where are you flying to? There is this world and the spirit world. They, those of great knowledge, do state, "You are leaving this world." That much we know, we agree on. Now we have by our soul entered into the other world—that of the spirits. This is where the disagreement comes into focus. I say the spirit world is divided into two properties: light and dark, divine and demonic, life and death, with Christ or with Satan, Heaven or Hades.

In the writings of our church fathers and the parables spoken by Christ written in the Bible, we find spiritual knowledge. In the writings of our world, intellectuals with worldly knowledge, we find worldly assumptions. We much inhale their breathtaking version of the life-after-death phenomenon and live our life with no depth, leaving our soul to prepare for its long journey. Our ignorance of the soul's journey is no excuse. In their writings, they, the wise, lordly men of today, movie stars—let us call them actors, because that's what they are—the same as many of us, just acting out their lives. Professors, professing out their worldly opinions to us so we may be dazzled by their brilliance, intellectuals that use their intelligence as a hiding place because in their mind they certainly don't want to be like you and me: not lowlifes like us. Their minds say, "As long as I'm so smart, I'm safe." Secure not in the spirit world, secure only in the limited knowledge of their chosen subjects. They live each day in the fear of the unknown, their poor soul waits in the darkness with the person's spirit held in prison by the same fear we just described. If only their spirit was set free to touch the hand of God.

Did you notice the resemblance of the rich man in the Bible and the writings of the two doctors Moody and Kubler-Ross? They have the same perception. The soul after death is going to be free to fly away from all suffering and half only self-realization, love, and understanding. The rich man said the same thing, "Soul, take ease and eat, drink and be merry." Just like the butterfly, not a care in the world, just fly away. But! Wait one minute!

The Creator of all worlds and all people in them and on them including Moody and Kubler-Ross and those like them said this, "You fool! This very night your soul is required of you" (Luke 12:20). God is not talking about the inheritance of the physical barns and materials the man has acquired. Who is going to inherit them? He, the Creator, asking the man about his soul, says, "Now who is going to own your soul?" It doesn't sound like a butterfly experience to me. It sounds like a spiritual thunderbolt, a clap of thunder, a bolt of lightning out of the realm known only to those that believe and fear God.

Somebody is going to own your soul. How was it prepared? Will it be Christ, the truth, the light, the divine, the heavenly spirit? Was it prepared for him the Christ? Or was it prepared for Satan, the liar, the demonic, the darkness, the master of hades? Is it full of sin and corruption? But Dr. Moody said, "There is no hell."

Well, let's go back to Luke 12:4–5. Christ is speaking:

> "And I say to you, my friends, do not be afraid of those who kill the body, and after that have no more that they can do. But I will warn you who to fear. Fear the one who after he was killed has authority to cast into hell, yes I tell you to fear him."

Don't let these people with their limited, worldly knowledge tell you about the soul—your soul! Prepare yourself. Start reading. Start searching. You don't have to believe me, find out for yourself. But do it with an open mind.

Father Seraphim Rose says of these people who get their information through mediums, "It is a teaching literally devised by demons with a clear intention of overthrowing the traditional Christian teaching on life after death and changing mankind's whole outlook on religion" (*The Soul After Death*, page 61).

Christ said, "Fear the one who after he was killed has authority to cast into hell." Now, common sense should tell you this is no joke. This is serious. Christ is talking about Himself, the one that was killed. Remember the cross? But, he rose again and now has the authority to cast into hell any of us. Judging is final by Him and Him alone. Fear Him on judgment day. Fear him before that day. Fear him now! For you who think this soul of yours will fly away in a higher state of consciousness and it's just an "unlimited process of growth" we try to explain. Do they see the safety in knowledge? Even after death they think they will be more knowledgeable. They wish!

What's going to happen to their butterfly soul as it just left its body, and Satan with his butterfly net swats their soul out of the air and sucks it down into His house and uses it for firewood, the kind that burns forever? Now who was prepared for this? Not those that thought higher learning was the answer. Christ said it, not me. Look at what my Lord my God said, "And who will own your soul." This is spiritual. This is truth. You, and you alone, make this choice. Who will own my soul when my body quits working and time leaves with death standing on my chest?

Have you heard of the old saying "The rubber has hit the road"? Prepared or not prepared, your soul, who you are, is going to its destination. Prepared, meaning the work and suffering you undertook to reach the light, the truth. Christ and the saints with the heavenly beings. Unprepared, meaning no spiritual battles, no suffering, not obeying any spiritual laws or standards. No principles, unbelief, and the like; the rich man take ease, eat, drink, and be merry.

The soul prepared means life.

The soul unprepared means death.

Your choice.

And the Angels Kept On Singing

And the doors of heaven opened wide,
(He/She) heard (his/her) name called and (he/she) responded,
Leaving all behind.
And the angels kept on singing.

(He/She) was welcomed by all of those who had went before (him/her),
Friends, relation, the known and unknown,
And the angels kept on singing.

(He/She) knelt down at the feet of Christ and flooded by the Light
    of His Divine
Being, (he/she) was welcomed home,
And the angels kept on singing.

For all of us left behind,
Know that our turn will come, our name is called,
We will respond and (name of deceased) with others wait.
And the angels keep on singing.

James L. Crawford

Chapter 13
The Soul

Trying to be as simple as I can about the soul is an experience in itself. After hours of reading, spending time alone with the Lord, listening to my mind and its voices, and in the final hours before writing on this subject, I find a great peace. A peace coming now from my own soul. I can find comfort now, released from the turmoil of the world by bending to the spiritual wisdom of the church fathers, the sayings of the greatest spiritual book ever written, the Bible, and to all of those who helped me on my way.

Thanks be to Christ my Lord for sending the Holy Spirit, for all of this I must depend on Him, the Holy One. To help me understand and have the ability to write to you these deep meanings. This is the struggle of life and death, between the Christian and the world, believers in Christ and nonbelievers in God, between truth and the big lie. Between heaven and hades and for all of us, every man, woman, and child, the last judgment day.

Now on this day we open the spiritual door even wider. Watch the works of the spirits closely for you are going to see how and why you must be to find peace and live forever. Let us start walking again down the narrow path. Remember, the narrow path leads us to the truth. Walking deeper into the forest, everything is still, and only those that live here watch and wait. Time is on their side. They do not have to expose themselves to us; they live here. Remember, we are the intruders. We are walking into their world, new to us, old to them, mysterious to us, home to them. But since God said, "I will protect you going in and coming out," then we know we are safe and in good hands. Stay on the narrow path through the wilderness, the forest, the desert, the mountaintop, the valley low, the swamp, the meadows—it's all part of our investigation, the realm of the spirit. From the high to the low, wide to narrow, and light to darkness.

This narrow path is inaccessible to people of the world. They cannot muddy this path with their foul-smelling water of vanity because they do not understand.

In looking at our soul, we must have and given great vigilance to this subject. We must give our whole attention to this above everything else. Go to your Bible. Find Luke 16:19–31:

> Now there was a certain rich man, and he habitually dressed in purple and fine linen, gaily living in splendor every day. And a poor man named Lazarus was laid by his gate and he was covered with sores, and longing to be fed with the crumbs which were falling from the rich man's table; besides the dogs were coming and licking his sores. Now it came about that the poor man died and he was carried away by the angels to Abraham's bosom; and the rich man died and was buried. And in Hades he lifted up his eyes, and being in torment he saw Abraham far away and Lazarus in his bosom. And he cried out and said, "Father Abraham, have mercy on me and send Lazarus, that he may dip the tip of his finger in water and cool off my tongue; for I am in agony in this flame." But Abraham said, "Child, remember that during your life you received your good things and likewise Lazarus received bad things; but now he is being comforted here and you are in agony over there. And besides all this, between us and your there is a great chasm fixed, in order that those who wish to come over from here to you may not be able, and that none may cross over from there to us." And he said, "Then

> I beg you, Father, that you send Lazarus to my father's house, for I have five brothers, that he may warn them lest they also come to this place of torment." But Abraham said, they have Moses and the prophets, let them hear them. But the rich man said, "No, father Abraham, but if someone goes to them from the dead they will repent!" But Abraham said to him, "If they do not listen to Moses and the prophets, neither will they be persuaded if someone rises from the dead."

To get the interpretive analysis of this parable, we will go to more than one book, because if all the writers find in it the approximate conclusion, then we can assume rightly that this particular mystery can be confronted.

By confronting death and the soul, we can, by processing both properties through Bible scripture and writings through the centuries of men in the church, find understanding and insight, but yet it will still remain a mystery. Those who have left us through death know the answer to this mystery. We who wait our turn know only that it is coming. For some of us, the answer will be here shortly, others of us have to wait.

According to Hierotheos Metropolitan of Nafpaktos in his book *Life After Death*, "God did not create death, but death has inserted himself into nature, as a fruit of man's sin and his withdrawal from God. There is death of the body and death of the soul. Death of the soul is the removal of the grace of God from the soul and death of the body is the separation of the soul from the body."

If we go back to our pages, we understood "grace" to be divine energy. Some call it "uncreated energy" in their writings, because it is God's energy then it is was before creation, because He is uncreated. Your soul and my soul must have His grace, His divine energy to have life. A spiritual life that will have spiritual knowledge and wisdom.

> In the text of the parable it says: "the time came when the beggar died…" and, "the rich man also

> died and was buried." Thus death is the greatest democrat, for it makes no exceptions. After Lazarus' soul left his body the angels received it and carried it to Abraham's bosom. Angels receive the soul of the just and take them to God.
>
> By contrast the demons receive the souls of the unrepentant sinners. The foolish rich man heard a voice from God: "You fool! This very night your life will be demanded from you" (Luke 12:20). The word "demand" suggests the demons, who claim the soul of the sinful person in order to control it forever. Therefore, at the terrible hour of death when the soul is forcibly separated from its harmony with the body dreadful things happen. The angels receive the soul of the saints and the demons receive the souls of sinners. (*Life After Death,* pages 22 and 23)

When we read about the bosom of Abraham, we are following the Church's explanation of the bosom being the kingdom or paradise. Remember the Lord said to the thief on the cross, when the thief said, "Remember me in your kingdom." The Lord said, "Assuredly, I say to you, today you will be with me in paradise" (Luke 23–43).

So now we have come to a point of understanding. Lazarus's soul is in paradise and the rich man's soul is in hades.

Below is something from the book *After Death* by Archimandrite Vasilious Bakogiannis:

> What is the soul? "Man's internal functions." The soul is divided into three parts: reason, longing, and passion. Before the fall, reason, longing, and passion were all directed towards God. After the fall the direction changed and they were turned towards sin and the Earthly struggle of mankind; now is to bring back and to offer to God the three parts of the soul.

"And God formed man of the dust from the ground and breathed into his face the breath of life" (Gen. 2:7). Amazing the soul is the breath of God! We have within us something direct from God. It (the soul) has something incomparably superior. It has spiritual qualities and when it has been cleansed of sin and of the passions, being now pure, it sees afar. St. Anthony the Great, who was experienced in these matters, informs us; "I believe that when it is cleansed thoroughly and stands in its true nature it can become clear-sighted and see more, and further than the demons, because it has the Lord who opens its eyes." So we have within us, then, something magnificent. A giant. But this giant is drugged. It is sleeping, snoring. We have given it a powerful sedative and it is sunk in deep sleep, indifference, indolence, inattention, and above all sin, are powerful drugs for the soul.

Saint Mark the Ascetic, page 37, states, "They will feel the unbearable pain at the hour of their death." He is speaking of anyone who neglects God's statutes and commandments and who does not struggle zealously for spiritual things. They cannot bear the terrible distress, because their soul has not been filled with God's light, His divine energy, His word, His love, His compassion, His forgiveness, and all of His wonderful spiritual enlightenment. What sinful nature does is fill the soul with darkness, hate, anger, murder, lust, carnality of all kinds; illusions, sinful imaginations, sensuous feelings that run deep in our bones and drive us out of control; depression and unforgiveness, guilt and insensitivity, fear and terror. Now the soul at the time of death cries out through the very properties it has been filled with. Love or hate. Peace or violence. If you have not paid attention to your soul, then start.

Every day talk to her. Be gentle and kind to her. Stop cursing her. Wash it with love and have compassion for her. Start to recognize her voice and listen to her. For you tough men, you macho guys that think you're so bad, I know the feeling. I was a bodyguard for a rich man. I pumped iron. I swore and cussed. I had a mouth that spilled filth like a large sewer pipe. I was my own law; I broke into a man's house and stole his "stuff." I was a thief. A man died and I didn't pull the trigger, but the trickle-down effect brought down guilt on me that I carried for years. Did I cause his death? Maybe not, but I was there. How will I ever know? These are things I put in my soul.

For you addicted to some sort of property, whatever it is—lying, cheating, beating your wife, beating your children, beating your husband, violence of any sort, drugs, alcohol, sex—they all have feelings that generate movement and body function. All part of your soul's environment. Did I write bad checks? You bet. Did I try to cheat the IRS? You bet. Was I a failure, a drunk, a washout? You bet. Did I end up with nothing? You bet!

And you women, don't laugh. Many of you walk around acting every day like your husband's are weaklings, you're the great authority in your family, you and you alone have got the final answer on all things. Your stupid husband is there for trash hauling and bringing in money, which he doesn't do that very well either. Your soul is filled with vainglory, pride, and darkness.

There is a word in the Navajo Indian language, "*Xaa beyoot holq.*" If you were to draw a picture of the meaning of this word, it would look like this: a louse (a many-legged bug) dressed up in fine jewelry, gold and silver around its neck. No matter how they dress, their nature never changes. I know some men like that. And I know some women like that.

I know one person real well like that. Me! The old me, who still hangs around waiting, coming back every so often to see if he can get back into the house he once occupied.

Some people get up and eat and don't drink. Some people get up and eat and then have a drink. Some people get up and have a drink then eat. Some people get up and have two or three drinks and then eat. And some get up and drink and don't eat. I know I always had my sippy cup filled with Canadian Mist on ice. I had my Bloody Marys before breakfast. If we were going to go somewhere, I might forget where I was going, but I never forgot my sippy cup, like a kid with a security blanket, dragging it around. It's hard to grow up and face reality; it's easier to live with the spirit of denial. He will cover for your addiction. No one will know, just you. No one can see inside of your house. And for those of you who do not know what a sippy cup is, it's a large glass or container holding your favorite drink like beer, whiskey, and water, whiskey on ice, any kind of alcohol. For those of us who are addicted, we all have our favorite containers, don't we?

We leave the world and its boring lifestyle and go into the spirit realm to find peace and truth, leaving illusion, imagination, and denial behind. Let's look at "sanctification." *Webster's Dictionary* says to sanctify means "to make holy. To set apart as holy, to make free from sin, to purify, to make productive of spiritual blessings." Our soul needs this sanctification, and it receives this cleansing by spiritual enlightenment. When our soul has been given divine energy, God's grace, and starts the cleansing process, this is the beginning of spiritual wisdom.

In your Bible, 1 Timothy 3:3, it says, "Not addicted to win, or pugnacious [meaning, combative, to fight, quarrelsome] But gentle, uncontentious [not quarrelsome not ready to argue] and free from the love of money [free from the demon of avarice]." If we do not struggle to free ourselves from the pleasures of the world, then our soul suffers in the affliction that these pleasures create. You and I both know the person that drinks and gets mean, gets drunk and wants to fight, be argumentative and nasty, wakes up the next morning and says, "I'm sorry," like that is all I can say. I'm sorry today, but I go out tonight and get drunk again.

What about the person that gets drunk and kills someone, wakes up in jail, goes to prison, destroys their whole life and their family life over what? For what? Just to prove what? Pride and vainglory? Love of self?

It seems so funny when I hear the addicted say they can't stop. For those of us who have stopped, our problems sometimes still persist and we try too hard to free ourselves by the grace of God. But if God's spiritual laws are too hard to handle and you can't comply through your sin nature because you haven't the will or the fortitude to do so, then how is it you will spend the rest of your life in tribulation after tribulation? Is it so easy to deny the spiritual life and yet you would rather pay your sin debt throughout the rest of your life with guilt, depression, lacking freedom, peace, love, understanding, a life, and all because down deep in your soul there is no life, you listen to the voices that suck the strength out of your body and make your mind a pool of poison? You poison yourself because to you, being glorious means everything.

But when the time comes that you cannot stand yourself any longer and your life is no longer "glorious!" then and only then can you change and be you. Our intellect is not glorified with Christ; therefore, we must hold our body and mind in contempt, not glorifying it but to put it under spiritual discipline. Start disciplining yourself.

If you do not know God, the love of God cannot be stirred within you and you cannot learn to love Him and His spiritual ways. Your soul and my soul, that is who we truly are, in there is where we find our real person, our real self. We must fight against the demonic powers that have trapped our soul by guilt and intimidation. Our soul is beautiful when it is illumined by the light. How will you know unless you put light in it and pull it out of the darkness? You yourself cannot turn on the divine light, but you can make the effort to start the process.

In Romans 2:9–10 and 11, Paul writes, "There will be tribulation and distress for every soul of man who does evil. But glory, honor, and peace to every man who does good," for there is no partiality with God. If you are not able to control your passions, that's your choice. Again and again I repeat and will continue to repeat over and over, passions are controlled by the spirit. The spirit of the Lord is the only spirit that has authority over those spirits that cause the passions to arise within us. And because this passion is powered by an evil spirit, you cannot control it.

Can you control your gambling? No. Can you control your drug usage? No. Can you control your alcohol consumption? No! Can you control your sex and sensual pleasure, and above all else can you control your mouth? No!

Go to rehab. Spend mega bucks on pills and homes established to help people with addiction problems. They can help you if you want to change, if you let your soul direct your activities. Not your brain or your body but your soul, it's your choice.

Remember, this is where your spirit is, with your soul. Unseen, unknown, and without understanding you practice the things that bring death to the part of you that is created to keep you alive. Just because you can't see your soul doesn't mean you don't have one. If you didn't have a soul, you wouldn't be here to be you.

God breathed into your soul to give you life. He created your soul to fit you and no one else. Now he gives you a spirit so that he and you can have a life together, yours being simple, peaceful, uncluttered, full of love, and able to see God's works within your heart and soul.

Remember Luke 16:19, Christ speaks of the rich man and Lazarus. Verse 23 says, "And in Hades, he lifted up his eyes and being in torment, saw Abraham faraway and Lazarus in his bosom," so the soul can see when it makes its transition from this world to their world. If the demons took his soul to Hades, then he sees Abraham, it must be the soul not only sees but feels also. The scripture says he, the rich man, is in torment. So now we know it sees and has feelings.

In the book *Life After Death*, it is explained on page 85, "The Lord says that the rich man saw Lazarus in Abraham's bosom. Not just the soul of Lazarus, for even though Lazarus' soul was in Abraham's bosom, nevertheless he is Lazarus, since hypostasis (body and soul joined together at the time of creation) is not abolished by death."

This is one of the reasons we will know each other as we journey to the other side. The soul knows the body and the body knows the soul. We are all different individuals at the time of birth. Not one of us is ever the same. Whoever has been born or will be born, all conversation with the Lord, bow your head, be humble, before your unseens spiritual father, the Holy Spirit. Call his name, ask the Holy Spirit to intercede for you before Christ, before your Creator, the Father God, and admit your guilt and ask for him to change your life, "I just want to be me." I'm asking, please help me change to be the person that I was created to be, not the one I have been acting like all of these years. Ask Christ to come into you, to cleanse your soul. "Be part of me."

Take your soul, this unseen, unknown, property of your life, this living being in both of your hands, hold it like you would hold your life, which it is. Lift up your hands arm's length and now ask Christ to cleanse it with his divine love. Purify it with His divine fire, fill it with His divine energy, His grace, and tell him, "This is my sacrifice to you." Today my soul belongs to you and will forever and ever, amen.

Lord Jesus Christ, Son of God, have mercy on me, a sinner.

Saint Isaac the Syrian writes about the soul in its journey from darkness into the light. Saint Isaac uses the word *aberration* now for us with a limited vocabulary and not of great intelligence. Webster says aberration means "1 a departure from what is true or correct, 2 it can be a deviation from the normal or typical, 3 mental derangement or lapse."

Our nature is inclined to aberration. We, many of us, cannot control our nature. Too many of us run from point A to point C, then back to point B and end up in point Z and have missed the whole point in our life. Some of you in denial would not understand because your pride and vanity hold your intellect so high as not to humble yourself to actually correct your actions and change your nature.

But because you have lifted up your soul to the Lord, you have given him your life. The Lord Jesus Christ spoke these words in the Book of John 5:24, "Truly, truly I say to you. He who hears my word and believes him who sent me, has eternal life, and does not come into judgment, but has passed out of death into life."

Now look at what Christ has just said. If we believe in the "one who sent him," meaning "God the Father," the creator of old, the ancient God of all creation, God the Father sent his Son Jesus Christ; and if you believe this in your soul, not just your mind, but your soul, deep within yourself, first you must believe what Christ tells you, and he speaks to us spiritually. "And you will pass out of death and into life."

It can't be much plainer than this. Now death comes to separate your soul from your body, which he does, but death does not have the final word and his hands cannot hold your soul. Your soul has been filled with the divine light of Christ, because you believed, because you are now you, because death has to stand there in defeat and watch our soul in it illuminating brilliance leave his presence and enter into the sweetness of Christ's kingdom. Life eternal. The Kingdom of God.

You have just left the physical for the spiritual; you have just passed from death into life.

Lord Jesus Christ, Son of God, have mercy on me, a sinner.

And so it is with the soul. Looking at it as a property, a being within us; a spiritual holding place, a dwelling of sorts, a place where all of your life experiences are passed through.

Have you been still and enjoyed a few quiet moments with the Lord, finding some loving kindness, and even in all of your suffering? Did you and can you still believe in the Lord? Is your soul soft and flexible in the hands of God, ready to do His will and not your own? Or is your soul a collapsed, empty, unknown, uncared for, unattended piece of lifeless spiritual property? Laying in the dark abyss of your inner self, paralyzed by the sting from your pride and self-love, your insensitivity, uncaring, denial, overeating, and just plain loss of all discipline in your life? Does the creature hold it in his hands and laugh, your soul stiff and rigid from fear and dread as it becomes darker and darker in its environment? It hears the hiss of death but cannot break loose from the evil of the past.

It's your choice, not mine, not anyone else, not anything or anyone. It's you and you alone. Today, as you read this, you are in the physical; tomorrow, when you remember this, you may be in the spiritual. Hopefully you will be with your "Creator." I pray for your choice is not the "Creature."

To My Soul

Be at peace, my soul, for everlasting to everlasting approaches.
Be at peace, my soul, for the Lord of Hosts has called thy name.

Be at peace, my soul, the angels have heard and they rejoice at our approaching.

Be still and listen, my soul, for loud is he who refuses to believe and goes into everlasting darkness.

Be still, my soul, and contemplate our journey. We shall see he who was crying in the wilderness.

Be ye quiet, my soul, keep your lantern lit and your oil ready for time will run its length, and you will hear the whisper of your caller, rejoice and be glad for your night has finally ended, now the eternal light is forever.

It matters not where we have been, on the rocky paths of distant shores the strong surf roaring. In the lush green valleys of great abundance between the mountains high and in the mountain paths some stones unturned, what lies beneath we'll never know. Those stones have slept in their quiet place since time began. The underside in cold darkness sleeps. The topside, the sunlight warm waits for the passing of each quiet day.

O soul of mine, it all means naught, it all has come and gone. The day has come and night prevails as you and I have seen, but yet the surf still roars and valleys, green rocks unturned, but you and I must leave.

Do not cry, do not weep, our time has just begun.

We leave this place just as it was for time will never end. Only you and I will part from that which was to that what is. Our walk to unknown heights doesn't grieve my soul.

Be still, my soul, and look not toward the past, for the rock still lays unturned. The underside is damp and cold, the outer side still warm, no changes in its present state will ever know. It lays this way since time began and stays this way until the end, only time alone can change its place for only time alone can change a stone.

Do not fear the trail, my soul, or I will feel the pain, the pain of leaving things undone, the pain of fear alone, the pain of fear will strike me down, so shall I be as the bottom of the stone, in darkness cold and wet with fear, stuck in times gone by, but know oh ye my soul that Christ awaits our final mile, and see his light shine bright. We will prevail as time has taught that no one leaves this life unturned my heart is not a rock or stone. I will repent, I will forgive, I will not leave alone. The angels now are here, oh soul, let us depart in peace.

Oh hand, reach out; oh hands of God; oh Christ, we are coming home. My soul and I rejoice. Our time is now complete.

Hallelujah

Chapter 14
Gossiping

It's fun to gather together for lunch and with others from the office or the same work area to talk about the "person for the day." Of course, she is not present, but her actions are a delicious morsel for our conversation on any given day or any time of the day, but preferably when we get together, you know, "our group."

"Do you know what she did? Who she slept with? What did he do? Oh no. He wouldn't, would he?" and the raking goes on and on. Friends and relations have no place to hide from all of us that have the "inside scoop." "I just can't wait to tell the girls." "The guys are going to love this when I tell 'em. Oh no, I won't mention your name. Oh no." And so from one day to the next, month after month, year after year, generation after generation, century after century, it never stops. Why do we enjoy "slamming someone else's door"? Why are we so interested in their life?

Do you understand "second-hand smoke" and how over a period of time you can become sick from inhaling what has already been in that person's mouth, down in their lungs, and back into the air we inhale? Therefore, if that person has a trashy mouth, I am receiving his corruption as he blows smoke in my face or in my presence. Would that person drink from my bottle of water after I had just had a drink and filled it with my backwash or saliva and spit? Of course not.

These are physical examples. We see the smoke. We see the backwash in the bottle. So we can reject this or that property by our refusal to be part of this place or that place or that occurrence. So what does this have to do with "gossip"?

Spiritually you are inhaling second-hand trash, consuming this or that person's problems or their actions, taking in the very sensuous feelings the conversation ignites your inner self. As the talk gets deeper, you inhale more smoke, and backwash are nothing compared to what you and I consume when we draw their circumstance into our life.

If your subject has some unclean spirits who are causing her or him to be out of control and you are thrilled by the talking and now imagining of their actions, you have just opened the doors to the their demons. The same demon that thrills them will come to thrill you.

Why is it that the woman or man at the office goes out and has an affair after being around gossip that promotes the thrill of this sinful act of adultery or fornication? And their life is never the same afterward. If they are caught, devastation follows. If they are not found out, then guilt will eat them and pummel them until they weaken and confess or may never confess but have a knot in their chest, a pain their soul that moans and groans. The spirit of guilt, he enjoys so much our actions to deceive and will wrap us up in his garment of pain actually caused in the beginning by falsehood and fantasies brought on by our previous conversation. This is not written to those that reject this compulsion to gossip and renounce the sensuous feeling of power and secret inner feelings that speak to us and say, "I know all about that person. He can't fool me. I know. I heard it right from the horse's mouth."

Gossip brings the feelings of conceit, self-opinion, and vainglory waits in the wings of the shadows, ready to enter the gossiper's soul, because the door has been opened to this evil spirit by the tongue. If you wish to save your soul from this evil demonic, then you cannot rest and enjoy the sweetness of love for gossip.

St. John Climacus writes in *the Ladder of Divine Ascent*, a sermon of Metropolitan Philaret:

> When we throw a stone up, it ascends until the moment when the propelling force ceases to be effectual. So long as this force acts, the stone

travels higher and higher in its ascent overcoming the force of the Earth's gravity. But when this force is spent and ceases to act, then, as you know, the stone does not remain suspended in the air. Immediately it begins to fall, and the further it falls the greater the speed of its fall. This solely according to the physical laws of terrestrial gravity.

So it is also in the spiritual life. As a Christian gradually ascends, the force of his spiritual labors lifts him up on high. Our Lord Jesus Christ said, "Strive to enter in through the narrow gate," that is, the Christian ought to continually work to fight against the passions of the world. He must take pains for his soul and his life. He must direct his life on the Christlike path and purge his soul of all filth and impurity.

Now, if the Christian who is ascending upon this ladder of spiritual perfection by his struggles and labors of bearing his cross ceases from this work and spiritual toil, his soul will not remain in its ascending condition; but like this stone, it will fall to the Earth more and more quickly until finally, if the man does not come to his senses, it will cast him down into the very abyss of hell. Whatever the outward circumstances of his life, the Christian must continue to force himself to mount upward; if not, then for certain, he will fall lower and lower.

Nonetheless, let us not forget that, unless we employ our efforts in correcting ourselves and our lives, we shall cease our ascent, and most assuredly we shall begin to fall. So as you gossip and enjoy the secrets, the tasty morsel of "their life," beware! You have just set yourself up for the falling away of your soul's ability to cleanse itself. Therefore, it, your soul, remains in a paralyzed state, being held lifeless in the demon's stranglehold, purely by your choice, by the words you speak.

Lord, have mercy on my soul.

AM I THE ONE YOU ARE LOOKING FOR?

Turn to your Bible, go to the Book of Colossians 3:4–8.

> When Christ, who is our life, is revealed, then you also will be revealed with Him in glory. Therefore, consider the members of your Earthly body as dead to immorality, impurity, passion, evil desires and greed, which amounts to idolatry. For it is on account of these things that the wrath of God will come, and where you once walked when you were living in them. But now you must put them all aside; anger, wrath, malice, slander, and abusive speech from your mouth.

The Book of Ephesians 4:31 declares, "Let all bitterness and wrath and anger and clamor and slander be put away from you, along with malice."

So, in closing, on the problem of "gossiping," you can see the kind of company you're keeping. Anger, now you tell me this demonic has no place in your inner house. Nor "wrath." No one has ever felt your wrath, right? You wouldn't slander a person, would you? Why, of course not! And that demonic "malice"? No, not you. He's not there either, is he?

Why do you think when you talk about someone else and discuss their private affairs in private or in public that you get this good feeling, like a sensuous feeling? The excitement of secrets being told and now you know all about it. While you're salivating over these juicy morsels, the demonics are putting "a hook in your jaw."

Wake up! These are spiritual no-no-nos. Can't you see that gossip and slander opens the spiritual door for those other beings to enter in and paralyze your soul even more than it was? They set and push your button from inside your house. That hook in your jaw has a spiritual wire tied to it, and on the other end is the demon's finger. One day you are yourself and the next day you belong to him or them, to put it mildly.

Chapter 15
Love

Because we must stay in the spiritual realm to understand our inner person, we must never forget the three areas of our makeup of our human nature. Just for a reminder—our flesh, our soul, and our spirit. How can it be that simple, yet how far we have drifted away from our true nature. We proclaim we are someone. The someone we think we are and live our whole life in a state of unknowing and misunderstanding the real person inside each of us.

What is wrong with this picture? We have our fleshly self, which functions daily as we go about our life. This is one-third of our energy. We have our soul, unseen and unheard from, but we all have one, it stores God's energy. That is one-third of our energy. We have our spirit living within the soul and is the connecting circuit to God's power—His divine energy. And this is the one-third of our energy, to sustain us spiritually and physically. So now the picture starts to take form and the master of all creation says in your Bible, John 4:48, "Unless you people see signs and wonders; you simply will not believe." Why don't we believe in spiritual discernment? Why did I follow the trickery of the deceiver? Why was I so conceited that I was constantly depending on my vast knowledge and my experience to get me through life, never satisfied, always looking and constantly eating the fruit from the tree of evil?

You and I, without Christ, are running on one-third of our power—our energy. The other two-thirds lay paralyzed by our ignorance and denial. The soul and the spirit are not functioning. Can't we see the simple picture before us? How long must we live by our flesh only? How long can it survive by itself as it tries to function on a limited power source?

Look at two brand new V8 engines, high powered and strong. The first engine we watch will be running on old used oil, thousands of years old, been used many, many times. The gasoline is mostly water with enough low octane gas just to fire the spark plugs and make the unit run. It runs and runs for years in this horrid condition, low on oil, low on gas, no one caring, but it is a subject of conversation at times. The world with its long experience on such matters could care less because it is so insensitive and cold-natured. This is our life without a spiritual desire, without a soul that can function and lay in sin, despair, cast aside, dishonored, and sick. The soul remains still and silent.

Why? Because the creature has been subjecting us with his poison. We have been running on his old used garbage, consuming his evil-smelling pus because the flesh knows no other way! We live in a spiritual world, keeping it hidden from view, and not perceiving its movements does not mean it doesn't exist. We are subject to the spirits that control our way of life.

Since the creature is in control, we will function in the flesh and flesh only. We will always be two-thirds short of all that we could be. That is why it is difficult to overcome bad habits, and those of us who add new ones will in time fall into despair and now we will not be able to benefit from obedience or discipline. In trying to explain this in a broad overview of our life without Christ and God's divine grace or divine energy, I'm sure the other crowd will scream and deny all of this, condemning it because it can't be proven.

There is a divine spark, a small amount of divine energy in every person. We cannot live without our soul, which holds and contains His divine spark. We are made in the image of God. Therefore, the human nature is spiritual and lives on its own free will to love God, its creator, or love the creature who stays hidden in plain sight.

In some of our previous notes we talked about the love of God, and I spoke of this to caution you not to give your God love to anyone, male or female. I'm sure some of us did not understand. Take your Bible, turn to John 10:9, Christ is speaking, "I am the door, if anyone enters through me, he shall be saved, and shall go in and out, and find pasture." By not knowing Christ, the mind will not comprehend the scriptures, spiritual words and sayings, spiritual phenomena and miracles. Your mind, you think will always be subject to its limited knowledge of such things.

Christ is trying to tell us He, Christ, is the door to our life, and we must pass through him to find the green pastures of peace, patience, and above all, love is waiting for us there. His love, God's love, not the world's love. Two different ways to "love," yet only one love to express our nature with. How can I truly express my nature, who I am in the world or who I am in Christ? You express your nature to fellow neighbors or family by that or those things or persons you love. If you love evil, you express yourself by doing and saying evil things. If you love good, then you express yourself in a manner of some affection and sensitivity, compassion, and a desire to help others.

Evil natures love contradictions, trouble, insensitivity to other pain, and suffering. Their inner self perceives the afflictions it causes in others and love the cold indifference they have for the one they hurt the most. Like the man that beats his wife and afterward brings her flowers. What do they all say? "I'm sorry. I love you." "I really love you; it's just for your own good. You needed that and I'm just trying to help you." Or, "I don't know what came over me. I love you so much." Yeah right! For you who live with an abusive spouse, there is a spiritual absolute for you. "Insomuch that nothing can stir an indifferent heart." There is and always will be in that person an evil spiritual nature, and it will receive some affection when touched, but it will not change. Nothing can change that soul's indifference. Look to your Bible, Genesis 28:16, "And Jacob awakened out of his sleep, and he said, surely the Lord is in this place, and I knew it not."

After fifty years of living with an evil nature, I woke up. For fifty-some years I was asleep, living and working and enjoying life, suffering, and at times feeling like I was suspended in the air. Here I was in the presence of God. "And I knew him not." Why did it take so long? Here I was in the arms of God for fifty years, asleep spiritually, and never knew it until I, by his loving kindness, awake, and like Jacob said, "Surely God is in this place."

Awake, sleeper; the Lord with His divine love will move you into contentment with Him, into a height beyond that is unknown to worldly people of all status. Ecstasy so wonderful that His presence causes an occurrence in our soul, yours and mine, that the soul, our soul, loses its solidity, its firmness, its stony, paralyzed nature and now becomes a vessel that has no limits, except the limits that you and I alone can, by our own free will, put upon her.

In our beginner's stage, we must direct our mind toward good. As we have said before, "Man's thinking, his mind is held and directed by the passions within him." To stop the movement of the passions that control us, we must move in a different direction for our life's sake. Truth and light are on the right side, darkness and passions on the left side. As we begin our search for God's love, we must look and watch our outward movements: what we say, what we do, and what we are yearning for. Start reading your Bible, start going to church, start talking to people who know, have hope, who are inclined to be truthful and humble. Try to be still and meditate on your progress to gain spiritual insights. Try to gain a mental picture on divine subjects. Meditate on your scriptures from your Bible. Stillness and meditation are your guides to your understanding of spiritual living. Your meditation, your thinking on divine truth, humility, and your new way of life in God's presence spiritually will start your soul to awaken. Now your understanding and meditation on what you read and talk about with other people spiritually will protect or screen your soul from evil thoughts.

The mind, yours and mine, when idle, will go back to its remembrance of its worldly past and will try to inflame the body, our feelings, with those passions we are trying to break free from. We must diffuse that passion or passions. Becoming spiritual takes time. Stillness takes time. Meditation takes time. But, all of this work shines a light on the truth. We start to become humble before God. In humbleness we come, wanting Him to show us more, bring more light on our dark side, stop the chills we receive from our familiar spirits as they create desires in us to descend to the left and its darkness. Evil and unbelief are waiting there. They watch our soul, twisting and turning in her paralyzed state in fear and horror; she, our soul, enters into their outstretched hands.

When I was vain and arrogant, full of pride and thought I was somebody, somebody special, it was not surprising that I could not understand spiritual complexities. I didn't want to and didn't need to. But, because I was an unbeliever and undisciplined, a hypocrite and blasphemer, I knew I had all of the answers. Then my turn came, and I fell, hard and long. "Thus sayeth the Lord, how long will you refuse to humble yourself before me?" (Exod. 10:3).

How long are you going to wait before you humble yourself before God, your Creator? Christ said, "It is hard for the rich to enter the kingdom of heaven" (Matt. 19:23). Well, it's just as hard for those who are foolishly wise, like I was, thinking, "I'm so smart." To enter into simplicity, in other words, when you are wise in worldly things you cannot comprehend nor even understand simplicity. How simple can it be to get humble and bow down before God? You can pray all day and night, and never receive an answer because you're not humble. That's why! When I had to make this decision, I said to God, "Well, okay. I will be humble before you, but I will not go out there and humble myself before other people." I still didn't get it. I still wanted to set the rules. I still couldn't enter into simplicity.

In Matthew 19:26 the Lord said, "With men this is impossible, but with God all things are possible."

"Is anything difficult for the Lord?" (Gen. 18:14). Today I want you to know I am humble before you, the reader before all men, women, and children. Before all mankind and, first and foremost, before God the Creator, His Son, our Lord Jesus Christ, the Holy Spirit, the very spirit of God Himself. "When you are cast down, you will speak with confidence and the humble person he will save. The Lord saves the humble" (Job 22:29).

When you and I will let ourselves be cast down in His presence, willingly or unwillingly (Job 23:2, His hand is heavy despite my groaning), we become spiritual servants, humble before God. Now he gives you confidence, and salvation is possible, and as time goes by His hand becomes lighter and lighter. And, some morning you will wake up and find yourself standing in His right hand and all of the oceans of the world in his left hand and you will be humble before Him and He will, with His fingers, touch your soul and gently insert his spirit, and you will be changed forever.

This is your beginning of a love affair you cannot comprehend. It baffles all description. This treasure comes from above. It is incomprehensible. The only way to know it is to experience it. If you have never tasted honey, how can I explain its sweetness? Pride and vainglory stand by your ear and whisper, then talk loudly, then scream at you as you contemplate taking on humility. The demon Pride brings fear in instantly to defend his position. "What will people think?" "All of your friends will laugh at you!" "You will be an outcast." "Nobody, nobody likes to eat humble pie." Why, when you have to get humble, you're going to feel so worthless and incompetent." On and on and on, like the broken record on the old Victrola. Like a barking dog, the spirits of darkness make all of these threats, knocks, and jeers coming from the thieves, you and I are subject to their verbal assaults.

Pay no attention, continue with your mind set on becoming spiritual. Walk past the barking dogs, and once past them you find stillness, peace, quiet time to contemplate your journey. We, you and I, must choose the spiritual love that lies before us, always within reach. Do we love the old self, the old man in us so much that we cannot change? Or, can we walk away from those that would devour our soul in their hate and anger for us? Can you walk away from brutish conversations? Can you walk away from the feelings that come from earthly affections? Do you feel ravished at times by unseen inclinations? Such raptures and ecstasies do not come from above; they come from below the evil spirit, your old familiar spirit who hides in plain sight. He's the one, him and his buddies, they generate feelings, but the wrong kind.

Take your Bible read 1 Kings 18:21, "And Elijah came near to all the people and said, 'how long will you hesitate between two opinions? If the Lord is god, follow Him, but if Baal, follow Him." Since love is our subject, spiritual love that is, not natural love from our sin nature, which is a lower love, a type of feeling that cannot be consistent in our life, sometimes greater than temptation, other times temptation is greater, and destroys love with its vicious concoctions of excuses and reasons of why we do the things we do. Your Bible gives you a spiritual look at an absolute explanation. Turn to 2 Corinthians 13:11, 14.

> Finally, Brethren, farewell. Become complete, be of comfort, be of one mind, live in peace, and the God of love and peace will be with you. The grace of the Lord Jesus Christ and the love of God and communion with the Holy Spirit be with you all. Amen.

This is the God that Elijah talks about to the people, a God of love and peace. A God of comfort and joy, freedom from the curse, from bondage of false teachings, freedom from the bondage of the flesh, doing only what the flesh wants to do, driven by the uncompromising mind. Freedom from having to put on our act every day, freedom to be our self, love God and to love him. The Bible's epistle to the Galatians written by Paul the apostle from the Orthodox Study Bible states, "Spiritual discipline is not a bondage. It is a rejection of the bondage, a pursuit of holiness which gaining freedom from legalism and sinful passions. The freedom of grace (divine energy) is known through the discipline of being bound to God the Father, to Christ and to the Holy Spirit. Saint Paul writes to the Galatians, 'Do not grow weary while doing Good' (6:9)."

Now we have talked on the subject of choosing God, which we have explained, His love He has to offer us through His spirit, His divine sinless spirit. Now let's look at Baal, because his name comes up now and then. For Elijah's question asked, "When," and stated, "One or the other." Taken from the *Revell Bible Dictionary*, "Baal, a Canaanite mythical God, dating to the 1400's before Christ." Baal was the chief god of sky and rain and fertility. In the myths Baal is portrayed as bloodthirsty and highly sexed; nothing has changed in thousands of years. The Bible identifies ritual prostitution as one of the depraved elements in Baal worship. The Hebrews were strongly attracted to the worship of Baal and erected local "high places" where his cult rituals were practiced. Not only did they worship him (Baal) to bring rain, but his worship justifies sexual excess, which appealed to many as well. So we return to what Elijah the prophet of God said, "Choose God or Baal."

Elijah's God is love, peace, strength and freedom, forgiveness and compassion. If you read the scriptures 1 Kings 17–19, 21 and 2 Kings 1, 2, Elijah stood alone in front of the 450 prophets of Baal. He was confronting the King Ahab and Queen Jezebel as they tried to establish Baal worship for the Hebrew religion. This time was in 875–850 BC, the place Israel and its regions. Sure as the sun comes up in the east and sets in the west, nothing in the spirit world has changed. An absolute. time means nothing in their world. This same thing is going on today as we write and read and work and play. Someone says turn to the God of love and peace; someone else wants more sex, more fun. Some find blood and violence as their religion: prostitution, drugs, and the spirit of temptation and addiction stand, shaking hands, laughing with the look of accomplishment on their faces, thumbs-up to Lucifer, the boss.

How long will it be before you choose God or Baal? A life without God is a life with Baal. For thousands of years this same thing has been going on, year after year. No sense for you and me to rush into anything right now. Take your time. Think about it for a while. Ponder on it. The demon spirit of procrastination certainly doesn't want us to make a decision and start our walk to freedom. Be your old self, just take what comes. To find true love, you and I must make a decision: force our self with all our strength, repent of our former sins and beliefs, fall on our face before Christ, and as the thief cried out in his last moments before being put to death on the cross, "Remember me in your kingdom."

In trying to find the secrets of God's love, I again and again looked and looked. Why did God choose this person or that person to do his work to receive his love? Why did God choose Elijah to face a king and queen and their religion, all of their prophets and all of their people? Elijah stood alone. How? Why? What did he have that I don't have? Why did God choose David to face Goliath to lead a nation out of spiritual poverty, face a king he loved and respected, and yet this same king is bent on killing David? How? Why? What makes these men become so firmly grounded in God that they have the intimate knowledge to do His will, God's will, His work, and why does God's will become the will of those He chooses?

Isaiah, Jeremiah, Ezekiel, Daniel, on and on, Micah, Zephaniah, and Haggi. Matthew, Mark, Luke, and John, Paul, Timothy, Peter, and on into the saints of yesterday and up to today. How? Why? They were human, so am I. They had problems, so do I! They gave up loved ones and possessions, I'm willing to do so! What have they done that I must do to make me at least a person that will openly and willing to be taught to do their will, for thou art my God?

So, I looked and looked, reading book after book, the Bible again and again and again. I lost count. I read the holy fathers of the church, the saints of old, history of the church and books on prayer, forgiveness, communion, born again, baptism, spiritual warfare, and on water and the spirit.

In my search for two years, the obvious evaded me. So simple. So simple. It's the "love" of God, so powerful a love it's beyond human comprehension, so deep it's fearful, such ecstasy that nothing on earth can equal its pleasure and pleasant feelings. It causes tribulation in the soul, because the soul cannot get enough and charmed by this divine love the spirit within us soars. We become indifferent to the world and all its glitter. When your soul, it being indifferent to the world, loves nothing the world has to offer, then your soul loves its creator. Our soul loves the divine grace that is sent to it from heaven. It comes alive with the feeling of divine energy passing through it. As the Lord's divine presence awakens it, our soul passes this divine pleasure to our spirit, your spirit, my spirit.

Our spirit comes alive, as now divine energy passes through the spirit, which then ignites the flesh with a charge of spiritual energy so strong it dissolves the chains of evil, unlocks our prison doors, stops all desire to sin, to live in the flesh, and wants his divine will to be our will, and our will is to be held in the arms of God. St. Francis de Sales in his writing states, "God's will is the sovereign object of the indifferent soul, wheresoever she sees it she runs after the odor of its perfumes, direction her course where ever it appears without considering anything else." The soul becomes indifferent to the world.

Death to the world and all its shallow pleasures. Life will remain our goal, and through this new life, the soul speaks its delicious influence into our feelings, into our imagination, our thinking changes, our brain no longer is the authority that has lied to us, reviled us, condemned us, oppressed us, we no longer want to linger in this darkness of evil; all of these spiritual properties bring us unhappiness and bad times, intolerable griefs. Prostrate yourself before the Lord. See yourself lying at his feet. Take your soul in both hands, raise your hands, ask him to take your soul and repent of your past life. Even if you're not a sinner, even if you see yourself above others, ask for forgiveness.

But, only if you want to change. Only if you want a total spiritual transformation. The simple secret, the very simple life-changing experience that Christ talked about with Nicodemus, "You must be born again." Through the soul, not the brain, not through the flesh but the *soul* and *spirit*, your total commitment to Christ. Then, and only then, can your transformation start and remain bound spiritually to the divine, unlimited presence of our Creator, yours and mine—Jesus Christ.

Book of John 6:63–65 says, "It is the spirit who gives life; the flesh profits nothing; the words that I have spoken to you are spirit and are life. But there are some of you who do not believe. For this reason, I have said unto you, that no one can come to me, unless it has been granted him from the Father." Again and again I take you back to your Bible. Why? Because all of our spiritual answers are here. If you want fleshly answers, read fleshly books. If you want worldly answers, read worldly books. It's your choice. Go and "click on" your computer and watch in secret all the things that ignite your fire. Your flesh loves it so!

But, unknown to you, you have spent your time, your spiritual time that you think is "your time" in the backyard of the very familiar spirits that can and will cause you problems whenever they will it. They call the shots. You answer the call to their will.

So, you think this is trash talk? Go and get your Bible. Lay it down beside your worldly books. Lay it down beside your computer. Lay it down beside your hot plate of food, your favorite dish. Lay it down beside your TV. Come on! Be honest! Which one will you pick up or turn to first? It sure won't be your Bible. Why? Because spiritual answers are in your Bible, and these are divine spiritual answers. Deep and profound answers. As you reach for your Bible now, identify that feeling of temptation to do something else. Anything—but not your Bible. "It just says the same old thing over and over again." An unclean spirit, so familiar in us that we think it is part of us, "It's part of me," being tempted away from the very power source higher than his own. The unclean spirit does not do this because he loves you. He does it because he hates you, and his cunning, deceiving power is generating authority over your senses, and with this continuous power of murky thoughts flowing through our system day after day, we cannot liberate our self from the temptation and secret thoughts which lead to passion or passions. It's called possessiveness!

Have you ever had a jealous lover/have you never had one so jealous that they wanted to possess you? You couldn't move unless there he was, waiting, wanting you and you only. Don't talk to other people. Don't even think about going anyplace alone, not even to the grocery store to pick up a gallon of milk. And if you did break loose from his chains, from his prison for an hour, you had to write a book, minute to minute, second to second, accounting of your time spent, where and with whom you were with. All because he says, "I love you." Bondage called love.

So what about God's love, his divine love that opens up your soul and lets your spirit soar like the eagle, waiting for the breath of the Holy Spirit to lift you higher and higher? So let's spend some time in God's love before we leave this subject, this property called love. Turn to Exodus 20:1, 5, 6:

> Then God spoke all these words saying; you shall not worship them [idols] or serve them; for I, the Lord your God, am a jealous God, visiting iniquity of the Father on the children, on to the third

and the fourth generations of those who hate me. But, showing living kindness to thousands, to those who love me and keep my commandments.

So the Lord Himself explains his jealous nature toward you and me. He, the Creator, says, "If you love me and keep my words in your heart and follow my ways I will show you loving kindness, by the thousands." "Loving kindness"—what does that mean? Your dictionary says it is "affectionate behavior" resulting from expressing love and acts of love, tender regard, loving care. "Love" is a deep and tender feeling of affection for or attachment or devotion or expression of devotion to and desire for God as the supreme good that all human beings have (*Webster's New World College Dictionary*, Fourth Edition; *Webster's New Twentieth Century Dictionary of the English Language*).

Listen, listen, the stillness calls.

> Wisdom preaches abroad, she utters her voice in the streets. She who is at the head of multitudes, she cries out, in the entrance of the gates of the city she cries out, her words, saying How long, O naive ones will you love simplicity? [Simplicity, worldly, not spiritual, childishness, naive thinking, acting like children] and the scoffers delight themselves in scoffing and fools hate knowledge, turn to my reproof. Behold I will pour out my spirit on you; I will make my words known to you. (Prov. 1:20–23)

It takes spiritual wisdom to understand God's love, His divine spiritual love. God said, "I will bring iniquity on those that hate me," if you love him or if you hate him. What is so strange about what we have just looked at? What is so different about man's "jealous love" and God's "jealous love"? Your sin nature love, or natural love, that is ignited by the flesh and brain power is limited. It can be overpowered by a demonic assault. Is the "love or feeling" you have for a person a carnal passion or a spiritual affection?

AM I THE ONE YOU ARE LOOKING FOR?

Before I met Christ, I expressed my love by human nature and its penetrations into the sweetness of sensual powers and the union of intellectual powers. And since I was blind to spirituality, I gave my soul and spiritual self up also. I feel deeply in "love" married, had four beautiful children, and in later years saw the shallow corporal pleasures as more desirable than the love of family and friends.

The ingredients, money, business stature, passions for booze and parties, friendships and unions with various desires seemed sensible and reasonable at that time. My appetite began by seeking more stronger unions with money and booze. Pride and vainglory came and lifted me up, higher and higher, and at the same time I was avoiding more and more my responsibilities, to my business and my family.

This is how over a period of time we lose our soundness and our righteousness. Complacency sets in and the inclination to "run" sets in, to perceive yourself hitting bottom just makes me more vulnerable to my "love" of booze and detestable, disgusting, inferior feeling of the downward spiral—that sinking feeling in your stomach and your continuous evasion of your responsibilities. I didn't answer the phone and didn't return phone calls left on the message pad. I didn't eat and didn't care if others did or not. I lost all interest in my home life and my wife, family, and friends drifted further and further away.

Lord Jesus Christ, Son of God, have mercy on my soul, a sinner.

So to try to explain God's "love" and our sin nature's ability to comprehend it; we look to our own experience with "love." In the world, without spiritual knowledge, love for each other is like human jealous feelings, sometimes higher, more sensitive and beautiful, sometimes lower and more beastly and painful. Our love for each other is a force of varying degrees.

A woman, happily in love with her husband, children, and her life in general, finds herself falling off the edge of the Earth. She finds the very one she loves most has betrayed her "love." She catches him in adultery and having given himself to another woman he has given away the very "love" of his wife. Never again will he be secure between her breasts. On and on, life in the world with his only hope of ever finding happiness, true joy and peace, looking and looking for "love." Many people live in a defensive mode, because some "lover" took their love and perverted it, used it for their own selfish desires, and haphazardly, being the animal that they are, destroy that "love" in a whirlpool of smug lies and deception, to put it mildly.

Because of these actions and finding no solutions for them, we, you and I, must turn away from the world's limited intellectual carnal life and, without a solution, empty-handed and lost in my own feebleness, your own sickness, we ask, "What is left," and we turn to the spiritual. I know in my heart and soul God did not make me, in his image, like him, for me to lie and suffer in this intoxicated state.

Saint Theophan the Recluse (1815–1894) wrote in *The Spiritual Life* translated into English by Alexandra Dockham, "As long as you are not living in the Spirit, do not expect happiness. The true happiness of man is life according to the Spirit which is the sub-covering of the soul. It is the means of communication between the world of the saints and angels" (77). Because you and I want to change our life or at least correct and heal the injured parts hidden within us, we must turn spiritual. As I have said before, it's an absolute.

God's love is divine; it is pure. Its sweetness described by St. Francis as the sweet aroma of the mother's breast to the newborn child, the child smells the natural sweet aroma of her breast because the milk is life for the child. It knows that life and its total security is in the warmth of the mother's arms and pressing the child to herself and the smell of her breasts cause the child's inner feelings to jump and pulsate. It finds the sweet milk of life and love for the mother pours out of her total self into the babe, her love. And love between the two is consummated day after day, week after week, and depending on the relationship and attitude of both mother and child, year after year for lifetime. This is a comparison of God's divine love.

This is why we come into the spiritual realm as babes, small children, unknowing and insecure, our outward parts expressing our strength, our inward parts mourn as they lie in the shallowness and darkness, caused by a weakness that only we know, each one looking for something and each one finding nothing.

We are children without the security of "divine love," and unless we humble ourselves and become children of His, the God of love, we will never understand. We must repent, my uncleanliness, fornication, my lewdness, pride, and vanity that say, "Oh, no, not me! I never have done such things." So in your sinless life, you, you were jealous, had outbursts of wrath, selfish ambitions, were a backbiter, your whispering of lies and false promises, you were never conceited. You never caused tumult in other people's lives. Well, well, well, and I'm sure you don't have the spirit demon of denial living in you, right? Give me a break! You had better find your knees, put them on the floor, bend your back, lower your head until it hurts, and say from your soul, deep within yourself, "God, forgive me."

Take your Bible, turn to 2 Corinthians 13:5. "Examine yourself as to whether you are in the faith. Test yourself. Do you 'not' know yourself. That Jesus Christ is in you? Unless indeed you are disqualified."

So if you look at yourself and cannot find Christ living in you, you do not have "God's love" and you really don't know yourself, then you're disqualified spiritually. You're not ready to receive His gifts, His blessing, His spiritual authority over sin and temptations.

"You are a land that is not cleansed or rained on in the day of indignation" (Ezek. 22:24). "Indignation" means, from *Webster's College Dictionary*, a feeling, or expression of anger at unjust, mean, or ungrateful treatment. Remember the people that cannot expose their spiritual nakedness, repent, or take a shower to cleanse themselves, but put on clean clothes over sinful, sweaty body and tried to enter the Master's house to serve him and receive the blessings from Him.

In our own stupid spirituality, because we are unlearned in spiritual love with the master, we try so hard to take our physical self into a spiritual world to gain our exalted positions, keeping great prizes of wealth and position. "I'm so much smarter than my boss. I'm so much greater and pleasant than those I work with. I go to church. I'm holy. I know the canons and laws of the church. I work and give my tithing. Why? Why can't I get ahead of those around me? I should be a supervisor. As hard as I work for God, and I have such 'bad luck.'" It is an absolute. Can you see what "he, the God who loves those that love Him" is trying to tell you?

AM I THE ONE YOU ARE LOOKING FOR?

In Ezekiel 22:30, the Lord speaks, "And I searched for a man among them who should build up a wall and stand in the gap before me, for the land, that I should not destroy it, but I found no one." So, since you're such a super-dude, so religious and known as "Mr. Clean" according to your own definition, why hasn't your Father chosen you? Why hasn't the Master found you among His servants? You're standing in plain sight but you can't be seen by your boss or your friends. Why doesn't the exalted one, you think you are, be put into a prestigious position? "That you would love it so."

I'll tell you why! Because if he chose me before I loved Him, if he chooses you before you love Him, we would build his wall out of "untempered mortar." "Oh, it would look so good," but it has no strength. The first strong wind of spiritual activity and everything would start to fall apart, we did not know the difference between "the clean and the unclean." Just try to make something stick to an unclean surface. Nevertheless, a property that is life and death questionable. Stand in the gap, before Goliath, I think not. I said before, when I was looking at destruction approaching my life and I had that fear, I had to run. The dark force is fear overpowering the natural instinct; it scatters our good sense and we have to escape, only unknown to us we lose all hope, and the gap is wide open for the enemy to overpower us—to consume us.

But when you and I give our love, our "soul's love," to the Lord, many things will happen, and before your very eyes, God's divine love now approaches, you will know the difference between clean and unclean; you, "who you really are," arise from the deep, your spirit will show supremacy over your natural needs and you will find peace and rest. As the child that sleeps in his father's arms, full of warm milk of his mother's breast, finds peace and rest.

When God's divine love, the love of Christ, the love of the Holy Spirit, their love, His love, enters into our soul, we are going to proclaim our new level of life, spiritual, with a soul and also corporeal. These three properties now are in balance, and the satisfaction of this balance gives you and me peace and rest. This is the "one thing needful" in our life.

In the researching and reading of the scriptures, trying my best to explain a mystery so profound as "God's love," "the love of God," "God is love," "Love itself," I had to smile and look more than once, because I guess it fits so many of us who rejoice when His love enters into us, and the consummation of His spirit and our spirit uniting is such ecstasy we can't keep our mouth shut, and we aggravate the worldly folks with our holy exaltation, becoming meek and full of love for Christ we accept the dismissal and the reality of who we are sets in.

"On that day your mouth will be opened to Him who escaped, and you will speak and be dumb no longer. Thus you will be a sign to them, and they will know that I am the Lord" (Ezek. 24:27).

Once you are free in the spirit, free from the world and its convictions, you will speak to the ones around you who want to escape, or have escaped from those chains of "utter pride" and "total arrogance," the world's satanic values. The church calls it "boldness," being bold enough to talk about spiritual fullness. Because you now can speak and understand spiritual knowledge, you "are dumb no longer." Before your conversion and your love of God the Christ, you only blasphemed and exposed yourself as empty and hopeless.

Look at the gang members, drug dealers, convicts, alcoholics, unbelievers, atheist, men and women, lost in turmoil and confusion bowed low to "Him who lives forever," fell in love, a deep love, and in return received His love, His grace, His abundance, His inheritance to give to those that love Him. And they talk constantly about Christ.

"Though now you do not see him, believing, you rejoice with joy inexpressible and full of glory, 'receiving the end of your faith which is the salvation of your souls" (1 Pet. 1:8).

You may not see him, but I have not seen him, but we believe and that is our faith, and our glory in Him so profound a way that we cannot express our love for Him to Him, with Him, without the Spirit, without His love for us and entwining with us in soul and spirit none of this will take place. You will go on in life acting out each day, whether you are a VIP or a homeless person, because the VIP can become homeless and the homeless a VIP. You, and only you, can, by your own free will, love God. His will shall be done, and when your will connects with His will by freedom of choice of both parties a love so profound will ignite and in your breathless moment, from that day onward, there will be joy "inexpressible."

Lord Jesus Christ, Son of God, have mercy on me, a sinner. Open my dumb brain and pour into me thy wisdom and knowledge. Open my soul and, with tender loving care, place your love in me and find in me thy temple, for you and your Holy Spirit, for it is my intention that the aliens no longer live there, but for you and your spirit only, from this day forward, forever, and ever. Amen.

> Here is love, not that we loved God, but that he loved us, and sent his son to be the propitiation for our sins, we love Him, because He first loved us. (1 John 4:10, 19)

> God loved us, even when we were dead in sin. (Eph. 2:4, 5)

CHAPTER 16
The Demonics

Saint Isaac the Syrian, this is his explanation on silence and stillness, from his book *Ascetical Homilies of Saint Isaac the Syrian*, "May I attain, my savior, to the wondrous crossing, whereby the soul forsakes the visible world and there arise in her thoughts for entrance into the spiritual world, and the experience of new perceptions." This man asks the Lord, "Can I reach a point in my life where I can make the crossing over from the visible world I now live in to the spiritual world? Because my soul rejects the world we know now and if I can enter into the spiritual world I can perceive (see) and experience a new life."

Somewhere in the Persian Empire in the early years of Christianity, this man who was once Bishop of Nineva cries out to the Lord. He wants to change his worldly life for a spiritual life. He identifies his soul in the female gender "she" because our soul is so soft, beautiful, sensitive, and loving.

Nothing has changed spiritually for hundreds and hundreds of years. Today you and I want to change our life, leave this ugly world of our sin nature and find a new experience, a new way to live, how just as this man did, without drugs, without pills, without any substances, just plain and honest prayer, just plain "truth."

When I lived in the world of my sinful nature without Christ, without anything spiritual, one of my bad habits as I have related before was "lying." We not only lie to each other but we lie to ourselves. Truth is not a shallow understanding to be frivolous and carefree with. Truth is found in the deep, the very essence of our soul.

When Isaac cried out to the Lord, he wanted a change, he saw some things that he didn't like about himself and he said, "Lord let me cross over to the other side." He knew in his soul something is over there that is good, true, and virtuous. His soul tells his mind to "shut up," and she contemplates her coming journey with joy and excitement. She, the soul, says, let me see and experience my new life in spirituality.

There is going to be a war within you. So be alert. No big deal. Someone is always around to tell you, "This will happen," or, "That will happen." What happens when you make your "crossing over" is the Lord's, and only His decision. But, remember one thing, nothing and no one can take your life; God himself has that power and Him only. Everything else is a lie or untruth. So, cross over. God said, "I will be with you always."

In those days of living in my intoxicated state, wallowing around in my own filth, I sometimes felt I was dead anyway. What reason is there to live just to contemplate my next move on someone else's weakness? And so what brings us into this state of mind? Why do we fall so low in our perspective that life is full of difficulties too great to overcome? Our struggle with our sin nature, unknown to us, weakens as we consume more and more of our impurities, whatever our addiction is, we love it more than we do our self.

Saint Isaac writes, "He who is accustomed to meditate on that which is evil will be deluded by the demons through a likeness of evil. For the demons assume a likeness and manifest to the soul phantasies which frighten her, employing for the most part the recollections of things seen during the day. Sometimes they quickly enfeeble the soul by a frightful sight of this kid which terrifies her; but sometimes they demonstrate to her the difficulty of the life of stillness and solitude and the like."

Well, well, so the naysayers resist the plain truth that we all live in a spirit controlled world, but by not being spiritually enlightened, they deny the existence of the very ones causing problems in our life. For thousands of years they have destroyed the life of men and women; they hide in plain sight. So Isaac relates to us the procedure used by the demonics, our unseen bearers of poison.

When you and I think about things that we would like to do and truth are evil fantasies, the demons are the ones actually drawing the picture for you, in your mind; you see something that is not real or true but in fact it is contrary to the reality—it results in deceptions. *Webster's Dictionary* calls "delusion" a false perception or interpretation. So you drive all the way across town, thinking and fantasizing on evil thoughts not knowing how you got to your destination, sometimes your fantasies assume the likeness of things you see during the day.

You know the macho stud who thinks all the women love him? The girl at the coffee counter smiles at him because it's her job to be friends and thinks love is sex, so he spends the rest of the day letting his mind run wild fantasizing sexual encounters with a woman than in reality could care less about the jerk! Of course, it's not the spirit of lust, is it? No, it's just natural. All in a day's time. If you were to talk with this person, he wouldn't admit it; these are his own private thoughts.

So since this person has never known the spiritual experiences, he falls for the sensuous feelings—his mind jumps from place to place, thing to thing—and this all leads to complete failure and despondency when it's over. Welcome to reality!

Did you ever know that a very small fire can melt a very large piece of wax? Did you know that just starting to read scriptures from your Bible and praying in silence, in the stillness of your surroundings, your heart starts to melt. Your soul starts to soften you can attain some sensitivity. You will stop looking down on yourself and your neighbor. Be inclined to do this every day, in stillness and silence.

As I studied and looked, trying to attain a spiritual life, become more sensitive and have a better understanding, there is always someone who says, "You're too sensitive. Get tough!" Sure, go back to the world, go and bury the dead and then go get drunk. Sure be on self-display but so withdrawn inside you suffer with your difficulties day and night. But you sure are putting on a good show for them around you. Who is responsible for your bitterness and sorrow inside yourself? Why are you sitting on your internal dung heap, your manure pile of the past? Inside yourself you are doing violence to your own nature.

Acquire silence and stillness, start your "withdraw" from the irrational thoughts, start concentrating on your scriptures, make friends with someone who understands the Lord and His works. When you humble yourself and ask about the Lord, you are lighting that small fire that will melt the large block of wax called spiritual darkness. Thirst for that flame, ask the Lord, "Make me a living flame of fire for you."

I urge you to let your tears be moist and tender. Cry, let your tears flow, your soul becomes like a sponge, and the cool water of God's divine love will gradually bring peace and joy, God's grace and His great cleansing power to you and your soul.

St. John Climacus in his writings on concentration of God's word says, "The demons fear concentration as thieves fear dogs" (72). St. John also writes on page 198:

> A friend of stillness is a courageous and decisive thought which keeps constant vigil at the doors of the heart, and kills or repels the evil thought that came. He who practices silence with a perception of heart will understand this last remark; but who is yet a child is unaware and ignorant of it.

Listen, be still, we are having a conversation with a spiritual enlightener, one who tell us deeds rather than words. Remember, look at stillness as a property, a form, and stillness has a friend. Its friend is a thought, but not just any thought, this friend of stillness is a courageous and decisive thought. This is a firm disciplined thought. It keeps the mind in a guarded position. It stands at the door, meaning the entrance of the thought processing what thoughts are allowed and what thoughts are repelled or killed before they enter into the mind through the door. This friend of stillness and silence does not allow the mind to be in constant motion, trying to satisfy passion after passion, desire after desire, wanting something but not needing it. Vigorously chasing the wind, letting unseen spiritual powers disturb your peace, and while they rejoice in your ignorance of their present power over your actions and life, you bear the burden and slowly lose your will to continue to fight; your desire for enthusiasm for life now diminishes.

Because you are a child in a spiritual environment, you cannot understand the depth of this message; therefore, you expose yourself to their indecencies. I'm sure you have asked yourself, is this all there is to my life? I just don't understand. And as we have said many times, God's divine grace is the changing power. That thought that guards the door is your spiritual discipline that you acquire from reading scriptures and your prayer time. It is well worth your time to investigate how by spiritual knowledge you can withdraw from the world that which was inaccessible, but now is within reach; you can live in complete freedom if you follow the straight and narrow path.

In our conversations of the past, remember that stillness and humility are virtues, and God grants virtues such as love and patience, along with humility, to give us spiritual knowledge and understanding. St. John Climacus, from *The Ladder of Divine Ascent*, said, "How can a man who is acting virtuous and religious think for one moment that one cannot see his pitiful disregard for the commandments and the word of God."

Why? Because of his, the man's, vanity, vainglory, and remember "pride," the stink pot. For all of you who have fallen that fall from the top to the very bottom and now live in disgust and dishonor, look back at your "pride" and ask him what happened. Pride will lift you up so high and when you think you are unreachable and above everyone one, everyone around you is lowlife, guess what? You just go your door slammed, and guess what? As long as this stinkpot is your buddy, he will make sure you can't recover.

Why? Because you have tried to live virtuously with pride and vanity like trying to water flowers and plants from an underground sewage pipe. Why can't you understand that the foul-smelling water of vanity withers water-loving plants.

In 2 Corinthians 6:16 God said, "I will dwell in them and walk among them, and I will be their God and they shall be my people 'therefore come out from their midst and be separate' says the Lord, and touch not the impurities of the world and I will welcome you." If you're going to go spiritual and want to change, then ask yourself, who of my friends can drive out devils? Who can raise the dead? Who has worked miracles? No one! St. John says these are rewards that the world cannot receive, and if it did, there would be no need for solitude; stillness and vigilance would be wasted time.

So now you have to think, who do I separate myself from? Well, number one, your old spiritual buddies. Start looking at habits that you have and you think are okay and how these same habits affect other people around you. If you gross them out and people find you disgusting, then maybe it's not them, maybe it's you!

Also, separate yourself from those people who do not want to change, and surely they will not comprehend your decision to move on into a different way of life. The sickening stench of addiction the demon who makes us fall daily, why cannot we smell his putrid odor, because we live with him daily, weekly, annually, year after year. He, addiction, despises God, disdains prayer; the addicted person regards the sight of the dead, as though they were lifeless stones, he just walks by.

Why? Because addiction has friends, like haughtiness, insensitivity, pride, fornication, despair, despondency, fear, gluttony, guile, and hypocrisy. Don't forget our old buddy suicide and more than we have named. We who have been addicted know these feelings have heard the voices that call us, wanting our flesh to desire the love for the body, a feeling that inserts itself into our flesh and wants this lower type of "love," below the animals; this love is a feeling of shameless and inhuman contempt, brought to us by a spirit that openly asserts itself into the very feeling of the person's heart and soul. God despises this lower type of "love," being lower than the animal; this love has not and never will have His, God's grace, except a small amount, enough to keep the person alive and that's all.

When trying to explain the demonic nature and his ability to infiltrate into our very being, we must want the spiritual ability to discern to see the troublemaker and detach our self from him or them. Once I found out that addiction was spiritual and physical, I then had to make up my mind how to confront the conflict. How do your spiritual enemies draw up their battle lines? How is this going to affect me physically, and will I survive?

Again and again, I repeat, you cannot go into their world without Christ the Lord only. He knows your weakness. He knows you are powerless, and until you acknowledge Him, His Father the Creator, and the Holy Spirit, the very spirit from God Himself, all is lost. You will stay in the flesh forever. The great Saint John Climacus, an authority on the demonics, writes, "He who has resolved to contend with his flesh and conquer it himself struggles in vain for unless the Lord destroys the house of the flesh and builds the house of the soul, the person who wants to destroy it watches and fasts in vain."

So you go to the man, pay him hundreds of dollars to be free from your addiction, whatever it is, and without the Lord, your money and the man leave you, never totally free from your problem, no matter how hard you try or how hard you fast you struggle in vain. Christ with His divine energy, His grace, will overthrow the demon's fortifications and destroy the demon's energy to control us. In the conflict that arises within us, we, with Christ's energy, His grace, now can constrain our self, constrain our nature. Because the flesh desires the flesh in our natural state, the natural state of our sin nature, the more we sin, the more sinfulness we desire. By not being able to constrain our self, by our self, the demonic, such as addiction uses this natural tendency to constantly want more and more of what we are addicted to. The flesh desires it and in its rush to receive that desire put before us, we slip into the pit, descending lower and lower in our fall, weaker and weaker, a burden caused by "pleasure."

Now the opposite occurs when we constrain our self, with God's power. We now have a constraining nature and it desires God's kingdom. The very nature that desired sin now battles with the very new stronger constraining nature to do right and to accomplish God's will in the remainder of its life. Right versus wrong. Good versus evil.

Take your Bible, turn to Matthew 11:12. Jesus Christ Himself speaks of this occurrence that is spiritual—spiritual violence, "And from the days of John the Baptist until now the kingdom of heaven suffers violence and violent men take it by force." When you want to change, to be the real person within you, then there will be spiritual violence taking place.

In the constraining nature I have received from Christ, I now confront the demonic who has had authority over my fleshly nature all these years. To cast him out, to break his hold, to weaken the very talons of this beast, I must constrain myself from his stench, his stinking breath that thrilled me so many times; constrain myself from his pleadings, from his threats, his verbal abuse as he speaks to me through my old friends.

"Well, come on, let's go smoke a joint and grab a cold can of Bud, then we can go talk about it" or "I'll be at the bar at 7:30, don't let anyone influence you until I get there." And, don't forget your sippy cup, you know, your whiskey and water on ice, the one you carry around with you all day or put your booze in a pop can; no one will know the difference.

In writing the description and other descriptions of worldly, fleshly talk, I will not go into the sensual voices heard from lust and fornication. Since you have a problem with lust, carnality, and such, you know his voice, you know what you think when you think it, plus that you enjoy those thoughts. So make a decision. Live with them or live without them, *your choice.*

Let's go back to constraint and our ability to say "no." When your friends or so-called friends want you to party down, get high, go out with someone else's wife, take on someone's husband that has been a friend of yours for years. She won't know; she probably wouldn't care anyway. Now's your chance. On and on and on. What part of "no" don't you understand? "No, I don't feel like it" and "No, I'm not going to get involved." Offer up to the Lord your weaknesses and let him fight your battles. The violence caused by your restraining against your old lifestyle is known to the whole spirit world. The battle for your soul is ongoing.

If you think Lucifer is going to let that happen without a fight in the spirit and in the flesh, your whole perception of the importance of your being has been neutralized. You are important. You are loved. You are worthy. When you and I can constrain our self, with God's energy, with God's will, with God's promises, with God's word, from the idol worship, whatever it is, then we, you and I will, no matter how violent the battle, we will take our place in God's kingdom.

The Lord said, "I go and prepare a place for you" (2 John 14:2). If they think for one minute that you and I won't fight for that place that God has prepared for us, that is waiting and has been waiting all these years for your soul, who you are, and my soul, who I am today, then there will be spiritual violence for that place in His kingdom, which is in heaven. A place called paradise. I will go visit in your dwelling place and come visit me in mine. See you there. There is nothing in the demonic nature that can hold you when you have divine grace within you.

"Truly, truly, I say to you, he who believes in me, the works that I do shall he do also; and greater works than these shall he do; because I go to the Father" (John 14:12). This is a statement, a promise, an absolute, the word spoken by the most powerful spiritual being to ever walk on this Earth; the most powerful, humble, loving, caring, human being that since time began has ever presented Himself to mankind, not only from heaven but also from Earth. Stop, think, what did he just say?

Number one, He, Christ, said, "Truly," that is absolute. Number two, He said, "The believers will do His works because He has to leave." Number three, He said, when we are doing some of those jobs that He left for us to finish, we will have His divine power to complete them and even at times to have greater power when the time of need presents itself.

"My shield is with God, who saves the upright in heart." When we turn to His divine spirit, the Lord becomes a shield for us against the enemy, and because we have faith in Him, He willingly frees us, saves us from this present, past, and future turmoil. And now we become spiritually like the infant, undressed and quiet, unaware of it; we enjoy our newfound freedom and peace.

Gluttony has just lost its hold on our soul and spirit. Our eating subsides and our hunger is for Christ, not for food and drink; our hunger is for the spiritual, not for the natural. Love for Christ, a divine love full of energy and virtuous habits, not the natural animal love that so many of us acquire but are unable to obtain its deep meaning, and we fail in our understanding of this paradox.

It is said by the desert fathers of the early church, "Better someone who has sinned, if he knows he has sinned and repents, than a person who has not sinned and thinks of himself as righteous." If you are an "eater," then stop eating! You cannot stop because gluttony, the demons, has his hook in your jaw and he leads you around by your stomach.

Sometimes "fat" means abundance and prosperity; fat of land means fertile ground. So the negative part of "fat" means overeating, self-satisfied, and more apt to abandon God. Gluttony destroys spirituality. It's his job. You cannot eat a big meal and then sit down and read your Bible without going to sleep, and if you don't sleep, then for sure you will not understand what you are reading.

Listen and listen hard. Gluttony is a demon that sits on the number two slot below Satan. He is extremely powerful. If you are addicted to eating, then he has control over your stomach. Why does he want you to eat? So you won't become spiritual. Take your Bible, turn to Deuteronomy 32:13–20.

> He made him ride on the high places of the Earth, and he ate the produce of the fields; and he made him suck honey from the rock and oil from the flinty rock. Curds from cows' milk from the flock with fat of lambs, and rams the breed of Bashan and goats, with the finest of the wheat and of the blood of grapes you drank wine. But Israel's people grew fat and kicked. You are grown fat, thick, and sleek, then he forsook God who made him and scorned the "rock" of his salvation. They made him jealous with strange Gods. They provoked him to anger, they sacrificed to demons who were not God; to the gods whom they have not known, new gods who came lately, and forgot the God who gave you birth. And the Lord saw this and spurned them, then he said, "I will hide my face from them, I will see what their end shall be."

This is not physical! This is spiritual! Can't you see what the demon does as he works to make us slothful, insensitive, and satisfied with our self? It wasn't the demon who brought you into this world and gave you your first breath.

God said in the previous paragraph, "I put you up on the high places." Those are the better places; he doesn't put us that love Him down in the lower parts of the Earth. God forbid. So we are put into a good life with God's grace upon us. To explain the honey and oil he talks about, I think His own description is better than anything I can comprehend.

> A land of wheat and barley, of vines and fig trees and pomegranates, a land of olive oil and honey, a land where you shall put food without scarcity, in which you shall not lack anything, a land whose stone is iron and out of whose hills you can dig copper. When you have eaten and satisfied, you shall bless the Lord your God for the good land which he has given you. Then your heart becomes proud, and you forget the Lord your God who brought you out from the land of Egypt, out of the house of slavery. (Deut. 8:8–10, 14)

So, look closely at food, it's on the TV. Eat and eat, people stuffing themselves, medication for heartburn from overeating. Don't stop eating, just take this product or that pill or drink this liquid, that way you can eat more.

We brag about the "good places to eat." We pay forty–fifty dollars a plate for food when we go out on Saturday night. Sunday morning we put two bucks in the church plate when it's passed, that's if we go to church. The other day a man sitting behind me was bragging to the group he was with, "I like to tip big. I left a hundred dollar bill on the table the other night." I'm sure this loud mouth person leaves a hundred dollar bill in the church on Sunday morning. Well, maybe I'm not so sure.

Why did the Lord Jesus Christ say we must fast and pray? This divine image of God who is and will be forever more spiritual than any who have walked this Earth or beyond at any time since man was formed said, "Stop eating." Fasting is cutting back on your eating, slowing it down, eating less and less, and praying at the same time you're fasting, day after day.

I remember when I laughed, I said, "This is a joke. There is a church that doesn't eat meat on Friday? They eat fish but can't eat red meat. Come on, get real, whoever thought that up must be out of their mind. Fast on Friday, I could care less." That was my worldly presumptuous nature. Years ago I didn't know, no one explained this to me. Eating tops our spiritual growth, and overeating is a way of the world.

But, be careful and do not misunderstand what is being said, "Fasting is not meritorious act, nor a way to win a more 'spiritual' rating from God or from others." From the *Revell Bible Dictionary*, "Fasting is a spiritual discipline, you make yourself develop proper control over your stomach" (374).

This is a sacrifice. Gluttony does not have a hold on my body. The demon hates discipline and hates control, and a commitment to bring ourselves into a spiritual life is his undoing. If you do not believe that the demon Gluttony has a hold of you by controlling your appetite, then "eat," enjoy yourself, and stay in your same old nature: stay overweight and stay worldly. Your choice!

In the Orthodox Church, on the fourth Sunday of Lent is the commemoration of Saint John of the Ladder. Taken from the book *The Bible and the Holy Fathers*, Mark 9:17–31, Jesus cast out the deaf and dumb spirit. "Healing through prayer and fasting. (813) For he who is praying as he ought, and fasting has not many wants, and he who has not many wants cannot be covetous. He who fasts is light, and winged, and prays with wakefulness, and quenches his wicked lusts, and propitiates God, and humbles his soul when lifted up" (propitiate means to win or again the good will of God). There are many good books to be read about fasting. Read and consume the spiritual aspect of this beautiful discipline.

St. John of the Ladder in *The Ladder of Divine Ascent* said, "If you have promised Christ to go by the straight and narrow way, restrain your stomach, because by pleasing it and enlarging it you break your contract. Attend, and you will hear him who says, 'spacious and broad is the way of the belly that leads to perdition of fornication, and many there are who go in by it. Because narrow is the gate and straight is the way of the belly that leads to the perdition of fornication, and many there are who go in by it. Because narrow is the gate and straight is the way of fasting that leads to the life of purity, and few there be that find it. Matthew 7:13 'The prince of demons is the fallen Lucifer, and the prince of passion is gluttony (the gullet)'" (30).

St. John says there are many who break their promise to the Lord. One of those promises should be "I will not over eat." Many people don't care now and will not care later and do not believe their eating habits affect their spiritual life, if they have one.

We listen to the spirit demon of gluttony who says to us, "Why are you, who are my underlings, overwhelming me with reproaches? Why are you trying to escape from me? I am bound to you by nature. The door for me is the nature of foods. The cause of my insatiability is habit. The foundation of my passion is repeated habit, insensibility of soul, and forgetfulness of death."

In your Bible, Psalm 35:13 states, "But as for me when they were sick, my clothing was sack cloth, I humbled myself with fasting; and my prayer would return to my own heart." Fasting creates humility. Why? Because it puts you in control of natural habits. Control of habits lets you gain control of the passions that rage inside many of us. You and I must gain control of evil feelings and habits known as passions.

How does this demon gluttony get into my deepest parts? You heard him—through the door of foods, our natural nature, he calls us his underlings. What's that mean? "An underling is a person in a subordinate position, inferior, scorned, showing contempt for authority." That's why he asks us who rebuke him, "Why are you overwhelming me with your reproaches?"

Once, I started to question this fasting and praying. So again and again I turned to the Bible, my spiritual guide, but also to other books, preferably writings from men with past and present experiences. The more I studied, the more I believed and in time used the prayer and fasting way into deeper spirituality. For those of you who laugh at these writings, as they are humorous to unbelievers in fasting, maybe you can tell me, what is Satan the snake using on Adam, God's creation, to make him turn away from God, God's principles, His statues, His commandments? His, Adam's, stomach.

God said in Genesis 2:15–17, "Then the Lord God took the man and put him into the Garden of Eden to cultivate it and keep it. And the Lord god commanded the man saying, 'from any tree of the garden you may eat freely; but from the tree of the knowledge of good and evil you shall not eat, for in the day that you eat from it you shall surely die.'"

The snake calls up his second in command and says, "Wipe your finger across his brain, light the fire of hunger in his belly and make his appetite so strong he cannot resist, do it, and we shall control him forever and ever."

Gluttony, the demon spirit, does as he is told to this very day; nothing has changed in all of these thousands of years. Gluttony, with Satan's shallow power of darkness, has control over you and me today unless we make Satan and gluttony our underlings. So before we can understand fully his power this supreme chief of our misfortunes, let's look one more time at gluttony and his position of rank in the evil darkness of the demonics.

> St. John asks, "Tell us, tyrant of all mortals, you who have bought all with the gold of greed, what do you usually produce after coming to us?" Gluttony replies with fury against us and foaming, "My first born son is a minster of fornication, the second after him is hardness of heart and the third is sleepiness. From me proceed a sea of bad thoughts, waves of filth, depths of unknown and unnamed impurities. My daughters are laziness,

talkativeness, familiarity in speech, jesting facetiousness, contradiction, a stiff neck, obstinacy, disobedience, insensibility, captivity, conceit, audacity, love of adornment and from these follow impure prayer, wandering of thoughts and often unexpected and sudden misfortunes, which is closely bound with despair, the most evil of all of my daughters. The remembrance of falls resists me but does not conquer me. The thought of death is always hostile to me, but there is nothing within men that destroys me completely. He who has received the comforter prayers to Him against me; and the comforter when appealed to, does not allow me to act passionately. But those who have not tasted his gift inevitably seek their pleasure in my sweetness." The victory over this evil vice is a courageous one. (St. John of the Ladder of Divine Ascent, Step 14, "On That Clamorous Mistress the Stomach")

Gluttony can and will become a passion. Passion is a strong emotion that has an overpowering or compelling effect and can overcome our power to reason. Being passionate means many things—showing strong feelings, intense violent emotion, expression of emotions, hatred, outbursts of intense feeling at fever pitch, sensual, strong sexual activity.

Webster's New World College Dictionary states, "Passion can be any one of the emotions, as hate, grief, love, fear, joy, et cetera." In our never-ending search to become spiritual, to change our life, and continue to gain and keep the righteousness we have gained through our commitment to Christ.

In the book, *The Spiritual Life: And How to Be Attuned to It*, by Saint Theophan the Recluse, his writings pour out spiritual wisdom, his thorough understanding of the soul, and this particular book is known as the "manual" on how to acquire a spiritual life.

> Passions as an obstacle to the spirit that burns with the love of God. They must be expelled. Your inner remaking will begin properly from the time your heart becomes warmed with the divine warmth. The little flame within you melts down everything and refines it; in other words, everything will begin spiritualizing until it is entirely spiritualized. Until the flame comes, there will be no spiritualization, no matter how hard you exert yourself in spiritual things. Consequently, it is a matter of acquiring that little flame now. Try to direct all your labors toward this end. Be aware, however, that the flame will not appear as long as the passions hold sway, even if you do not indulge them. Passions are like dampness in firewood. Damp firewood does not burn. It is necessary to fetch dry logs from somewhere and kindle them. Once they start burning, they begin drying out the dampness, and depending on how much they are able to dry the damp firewood they set it afire. Thus the fire drives out the dampness and spreads, and all the wood is engulfed by flames.
>
> Our firewood consists of all the faculties of our souls and all the functions of our bodies. All of these, so long as the person does not pay attention to himself, are saturated with dampness with passions, that is, and, until these passions are driven away, they stubbornly resist the spiritual fire. Recall how when I described to you what is inside us, I wrote that there is within us a kind of chaotic, stormy region in which thoughts, and desires and emotions are jumbled in confusion and scattered by passions like dust. I situate this

region between the soul and body. Stipulating that the passions do not belong to our nature but are alien to it. They do not remain inside the gap, however, instead, they pass right into both soul and body and place the spirit itself-the consciousness and free will—under their power, and in this way rule the entire person. When they work in collusion with the demons, the demons rule through them over the person who nevertheless thinks that he himself is in control.

It is the spirit that first of all escapes from these bonds. The grace of God pulls it free. The spirit filled with the fear of God by action of grace, breaks off any ties with the passions and, repenting for what has passed, makes a firm commitment from this point forward to please God alone and to live for him alone walking in his commandments. The spirit, standing fast in its resoluteness, then drives the passions from the soul and body with the help of divine grace, and everything inside becomes spiritualized. (Chapter 53)

So now you and I can look at what drives us to do what we do, and why we do it, when we do it. Remember stillness, stop the emotions, stop the clattering and constant bombardment of noise and motions. "Be still and know that I am God." Your Creator said it; I'm just repeating what He said.

It's spiritual to be still, to stop, to contemplate and listen to your soul. Shut your mind down by being still. The mind hates for you to be still; it hates stillness. Why? Because emotion cannot control the body through its passions, and the demons must wait to see what's coming next. Confusion is one of their power sources. The flame is the Holy Spirit, and, he will not come into the home of noise and confusion. So before the divine energy, or grace, can be given to you to start your spiritual engine, you have to find stillness and humbleness. In this quiet time we find repentance. We repent of our sins, and the Holy Spirit moves sin to help us subdue this dog gluttony by prayer and fasting, repentance of our sins, and meditating on him who is above nature and cleaning our house with divine grace given to us by Christ through the Holy Spirit.

Our spirit, yours and mine, must escape the sensuous "feel good" passion. Stop listening to the lie that "I can do it by myself."

Saint John Climacus in his writings, page 104, of *The Ladder of Divine Ascent*, states, "For it is impossible for anyone to conquer his own nature. For beyond dispute, the weaker gives way to the stronger." Christ, who is above all things created, is the only one who can change our nature and that must be by our own willingness to receive Him, and He sending the Holy Spirit to us now gives us meaning to the scriptures John 3:5–6, "Except a man be born of water and of spirit he cannot enter into the Kingdom of God; for only that which is born of the spirit is spirit." Because our passions are holding our nature, our soul and body under their authority, we are the weaker, they the stronger. Now comes the Holy Spirit injecting divine energy into our spirit, and now because divine energy is higher and stronger than anything the darkness has in its arsenal, we can by our spirit start to acquire love and fear of God, which in turn makes the passion weaker and our ability to conquer it and our corruptible body, now a very good foothold, has taken place for the beginning of change within our self.

It has been over a week now since I have been able to write. Time passes on and does not wait. Today is cold outside, 15° and a very light snow is falling. The fireplace is burning and the wood stove is hot here in the house and the wood heat feels good to my old bones. It is very quiet outside and very quiet here in the basement of our home.

And so I come to you without fanfare, without the drums beating and bells ringing. There is only the noise of the pen as it moves across my paper. The years have passed by, and the days and weeks seem like yesterday since I started to write to you about a spiritual life, and here we are on the subject that for some brings fear, and others unbelief, and others anxiousness, and some find peace and joy because it confirms feelings that could not be understood otherwise.

AM I THE ONE YOU ARE LOOKING FOR?

There was a man back in the 1930s when Germany was growing into a menace who tried to alert British elites, politicians, that Germany was a trouble, a problem on the horizon. The man's name was Winston Churchill and he appealed in vain for Britain and America to rearm. A war was coming, something terrible is taking place, and we must prepare and be ready. His voice was alone in the wilderness of sophisticated and secularized politicians. History has shown they did not listen.

In some writings it was said they were amused at his assertions and others a complete disregard of what was taking place around them. Winston Churchill thought of a poem, its author unknown, that fits his situation at that time, and it goes like this:

> Who is in charge of the clattering train?
> The axles creak and the couplings strain,
> the pace is hot and the points are near
> and sleep has deadened the driver's ear.
> The signals flash through the night in vain,
> for Death is in charge of the clattering train.

How many times do we hear the conductors who stand by the waiting train, all dressed up to look and act like we should follow their lead as they cry "All aboard!" There sits the train in your life, all shined up and polished bright and clean. You can hear the hiss of the brakes and the hydraulics and ready for the lever to be pushed. The seats so soft and the ride so smooth, just sink down into the luxury of the ride. Life is good. Get on this train. It's party time and it's time to let your hair down, uninterrupted years full of experiencing freedom, money, tables full of food as far as you can see, women, men, children, material wealth unlimited, intellectual assets that make your life so easy and will bring you fame and glory, uninterrupted sexual pleasure.

The conductors stand in their polished boots, pressed shirts and pants, gold buttons on their jackets, their ties tied in a perfect knot, and our passion jump inside of us as we crowd to the platform with our baggage and we hear the familiar call. "All aboard!"

And now today after losing everything in my life then and to regain my life again now, I can say one thing: run, run real fast, run as fast as you can when you see that train pulling into your station, when your passions cry out "all aboard," run fast and far, far away.

Many of us have ridden this train as addicts, addicted to one form or another. The demon with his hold on my life, wiping his filthy finger across my brain, telling me, "I have a whole lifetime ahead of me, fifty or sixty years of regenerating energy. Go for it." "All aboard!"

I realized later as I stood and looked at the train wreck around me that this was. How many people do you know that, not including yourself, have boarded this clattering train and have had their lives destroyed?

I don't have to name the subject that caused it, for everything subject to decay loses its value, and causes a downward fall. There is not one thing sinful that will not decay in time; it will lose its value, find those of us that are not in denial will confirm that as one sin decays two or more worse than the one that lost its value comes to take its place. To gain control of our life, our train wreck, we must endure a prolonged process called "self-emptying."

Remember when we said there is only one "absolute being," Father God through Jesus Christ. No matter where you live, how you live, how rich, or how poor, you will never be aware of your nothingness and the squalor you live in until you become aware of the sonship to God the Father through Christ, and start a spiritual journey.

It is terrifying to look at who I thought I was and the intensity of my stupidness to try to be that someone, the someone I knew I could be if I tried, and I tried hard, so hard I was ignorant to the state, the spiritual state, around me. In the book *We Shall See Him as He Is* by Archimandrite Sophrony, it states, "The roots of the 'knowledge of evil' grow deep and are not torn up of one's own strength. Those who are ignorant of this state of the spirit will never understand" (19).

He is saying as long as we are not in a spiritual state, then we cannot understand our state of being and therefore will be unable to, by our own strength, bring our self out of our sufferings, and our sin nature will remain the authority over our being, our state of being.

This clattering train is not the only voice of the world and all of its opinions but the voices of the demons around us as we try to function in our everyday life. In those years, my state of being was a state of dysfunction, dysfunctional though processing. My passions came first. I knew nothing of spirituality or truth, religion was a mockery, temptation was my friend, stubbornness was my best adviser, and being numb and zoned out was a way of life for me in those days.

I'm sure the reader of this book knows the good, the bad, and the ugly of their own heart, but what is shocking and so terrifying is when we decide to change our life and are determined to purchase peace at tall costs, we experience the greatest trial of our lives, and through that trial we begin to see how much of a hold the darkness of the creature's world has had on us.

The more we turn to the Lord and receive his spirit in us, the more we will have understanding and the concept to prevail and maintain. Whoever wrote "death is in charge of the clattering train" knew full well that our life was in danger, if we rode this train. By the way, who's in charge of clattering train? Vainglory, a spirit who can be identified by having a bitter experience with, is the fault of self-centeredness.

I regret in my old age the years I spent with this demon. When I really thought I was somebody, I was not the "respecter of persons" nor was I in any way understandable to those that were fainthearted. As we have stated before, his demon cannot be perceived and evicted without the Lord's help. Some of what we write may be repetitious, so don't become bored but try to understand the primary reason we are giving this subject a special place.

From *The Ladder of Divine Ascent,* Step 11, it states, "If any one were to try to philosophize at length on this subject, he would be like someone who vainly troubles himself over the weight of the winds" (132). Looking at Vainglory as a property, a spirit being, a demon that brings about the beginning of passions, he is known as unholy self-esteem. When he enters into us, he changes our nature; he is a perversion of our character. Saint John writes about this demon with an openness and such simplicity that I cannot put the entire chapter on paper.

A vainglorious person is a believing idolater; a person who apparently honors God but he wants to please men more than God. He is a lover of self-display. Some men fast and pray, but because he loves his inner feeling of self-display and the joy it brings him in his nature. Vainglory speaks to him and says, "They are watching you. They think you are so holy. Oh, you are so righteous, so upright and noticeable." His inner voice makes you tremble with the passion of pride.

But the man exults. His body, his prayers are futile, and his fasting is without reward his prayers fall dead at his feet because he has done it all for the praise of men. Vainglory, the demon, has cheated the man out of his reward and he has exhausted his body, for God does not honor the man who is led by the demon, who pronounces you so blessed.

Remember that the old saying, "Flattery will get you nowhere." Don't receive praise unless you give it to God. The next time someone praises you, you return it with "God is good." You and I must continue to reject the praise of the demons. We must show our humility and maintain our love for Christ our God.

Remember vainglory when he whispers to you, "Set out in order to save the souls which are perishing." Vainglory rebukes subordinates mercilessly. I'm sure you know the boss who makes an effort to belittle his employees. The man or woman with the demon is always preferred, always proud, and when they are the least bit slighted, they become resentful.

Anger also is a coworker with vainglory, but when a bad temper is hurling a man to destruction, vainglory jumps in and can instantly change the man's intention, because he wants the praise of worldly glory. Because this particular paragraph must be read in its entirety, I quote page 135, paragraph 31:

> He who is proud of his natural advantages, I mean cleverness, ability to learn, skill in reading, a clear pronunciation, quick understanding and all such gifts received by us without labor, will never obtain supernatural blessings, because he who is unfaithful in a little is also unfaithful and vainglorious in much.

"There is glory that comes from God, from our Lord, for he says 'those that glorify me, I will glorify'" (Kings 11:30).

When the Lord thinks you and I are ready for his favor to fall on us, His glory, it will, and make no mistake about it. When the absolute God, the Father God of all Christians, speaks through this writings of our Bible, His absolute word is truth and He will glorify you if you believe, if you repent, if you obey His word and commandments.

Vainglory, the demon spirit, is the mother of the demon Pride, the spirit causing proud evil desires inside of us, into our very being. No matter how trifling the feeling is, you will know because you are hoping to be seen and observed by other men and women.

Pride, this demonic devil, has its own children, and one is arrogance. With arrogance, the passion of pride introduces the passion to the victim. It is instantaneous and swifter than it can be noticed and, sometimes unknown to the victim, enters the soul, and because of bodily sense, evil thoughts are born.

So when the demon spirit of vainglory continues to increase, it then gives birth to pride. "Pride," Saint John says, "is the origin and the consummation of all evils." Step 23, *The Ladder of Divine Ascent*, "On Mad Pride and on Unclean Blasphemous thoughts:

> Pride is denial of God, an invention of the devil, the despising of men, the mother of condemnation, the offspring of praise, a sign of sterility (producing little or nothing, unfruitful), flight from Divine assistance, the precursor of madness, the cause of falls (spiritual), a foothold for satanic possession, a source of anger, a door of hypocrisy, the support of demons, the guardian of sins, the patron of pitilessness, the rejection of compassion, a bitter inquisitor, an inhuman judge, an opponent of God, a root of blasphemy. (138)

Be very much aware of this feeling. The above should make us aware because it in itself describes feelings that all of us have had at one time or another. It finds food in gratitude, because the passion is not above self-praise in the heart and does not always advise us to deny God. Remember the Pharisee in the Book of Luke 18:11, "The Pharisee stood and prayed thus with himself, 'God, I thank You that I am not like other men—extortioners, unjust, adulterers, or even this tax collector.'"

But Christ said in verse 14, "For every one who exalts himself shall be humbled and he who humbles himself shall be exalted." So you see, they stand in church and thank God out loud, but they mentally magnify themselves.

The falling away from God is a willingness of the man for pride to come, and he does, quickly. He, pride, will pitch his tent at your place and will bring passion after passion after passion, and the stronger this demon spirit becomes, the more evil you become. The stronger are the passions. Saint John says, "A proud man is like a pomegranate, rotten inside while outwardly radiant with beauty. I do not know how it is, but the majority of the proud remain ignorant of their real selves. They imagine that they are free from all passions, ("I am not a sinner!") and the only time they realize they have a need, they lack spirituality, they are in poverty, is at the departure of this life."

So in conclusion, to pride and vainglory we shall run to or run from; our choice, yours and mine. But remember their offspring, the fall of spiritual mean, anger, calumny, spite, irritability, shouting, blasphemy, hypocrisy, hatred, envy, disputation (fond of arguing), self-will, and disobedience. These spirits all oppose God and His commandments, His statutes and His word, our Lord Jesus Christ.

If the day comes when you believe these things then start with your self-emptying, keep up a sincere condemnation of these sins before the Lord. Become humble before God and repent. Learn spirituality by finding yourself in true prayer. Stretch out your hands, raise your hands to heaven, deep sighing, firmness of mind; do not let them take your mind and spin it, for they choose to attack us at this very time.

Cry out to the Lord, not in clever words but in humble words, "Have mercy on me for I am weak and frail, and when my lamp of faith goes out, I falter and I fail."

"Lord Jesus Christ, Son of God, have mercy on me, a sinner."

If you cannot think of what to say as times goes by, then repeat the above Jesus prayer, "Lord Jesus Christ, Son of God, have mercy on me, a sinner." This prayer is used and has been used for thousands of years by the Orthodox Church. The monks and nuns continually pray this prayer throughout their life. Very simple, yes. Very powerful, yes. So powerful books have been written on it.

So if we look at vainglory as the horse and pride being in the saddle, we can, with our holy humility and our self-accusations before God, laugh at both the horse and its rider, for we can now sing the victory song to the Lord, "Let us sing to the Lord; for gloriously is he glorified: horse and rider hath he hurled into the sea," and into the abyss of humility.

Then you will know by the experience the power of the most high, and with invisible help you will invisibly drive away the invisible ones. He who accustoms himself to wage war in the way will soon be able to put his enemies to flight solely by spiritual means, for the latter is a recompense from God to the doers of the former, and rightly so.

An absolute God who changes us to our true selves, by His invisible divine grace, power from on high, He bestows on those that fear Him and love Him.

> I fall down before the compassion of thy kindness, O master of all! Accept the prayer of a sinner; sweeten my soul which languishes in the bitterness of sin. Give me a drink, when I am thirsty, from the fountains of life and guide me along its path.
>
> As my master, rescue me, thy slave, from captivity, that I might be freed from slavery to the dishonorable passions that have entangled my heart. May the compassion forestall me before I am dragged down to hell together with those who work iniquities.

At that time all that I do now in darkness will be made manifest. Woe is me; what shame will embrace me when those who now think I am irreproachable see me condemned, when they see how I, who is miserable, have neglected spiritual deeds and labored for the passions. Woe is me! O my soul, why is the sun of your mind clouded by the haze of passions? And why does this haze not disappear when rays of light shine forth? Why do you allow the passions to drag you down to the Earth, and why have you preferred bonds over freedom? The garment God wove for you, have you made unfit for use and use unworthy for the royal wedding. Willingly have you given yourself up to sin and enslaved yourself to the enemy of life.

What will you say to the judge in that day of fear and trembling? Come to your senses, while there is still time. While you are still the mistress of your thoughts, while your mind is still functioning. While there is yet movement in your body, while it is still possible for grace to touch your heart, and while you can still shed cleansing tears—take a brave step and stand against the passions and, with God's help, valiantly smite Goliath.

Hurry, do not let a thief outrun you, do not let a harlot reach the entrance before you, do not let one of the violent who take the Kingdom of God by force block the door. Hurry, for when the contest is over, it is no longer possible to enter competitions. When the market is closed, it is not possible to seek goods, and when a transaction is completed, it is not possible to take part in it. While there is time, hurry to engage in battle, that you might overcome your enemies and show yourself worthy to receive a crown.

This was the prayer from *The Spiritual Psalter*, "Hasten to Correct Yourself While There is Still Time."

And so from many different walks of life we come, but tormented by many for some and tormented by a few for others, but they are always the same ones. The tormentors will remain the same forever until the last day, until Christ comes to earth, and the house cleaning will start. "Lord Jesus Christ, come today to start in my house." Amen.

Now, just to be clear and open about the Lord's coming, we know from scriptures throughout the Old and New Testament that there will be a house cleaning when he returns. The final time comes in the verses of Revelation 20:10, "The devil, who deceived them was cast into the lake of fire and brimstone where the beast and the false prophet are." So that part of the house is cleaned, and in verse 14, same chapter, it says, "Then Death and Hades were cast into the lake of fire."

Now all parts of the house have been cleaned and ready for the tabernacle of God. And just as we see this cleansing taking place, we should not rule out verse 15, same chapter, "And anyone not found written in the book of life was cast into the lake of fire." In all of the spiritual writings that I have read, there is only one route of escape: this road is not well traveled, this road is filled with stumbling blocks, and this road ends in the book of life.

Of all the saints, of all the pastors, priests, and those that follow the spiritual path, from out of the Bible, the Word of God, there is the beginning and the end.

Conclusion
Repentance

Telling the Lord everything—the good, the bad, and the ugly—the ugly hurts the worst, the bad hurts bad enough, and the good evil. Think about it! What's been good to you is evil to Him, so get it all out. All of the demonics hate this one action. This action takes determination, truthfulness, and sorrow. It's going to hurt, it's going to take you down a road, leaving Satan's junk alley, his territory where he has had victory after spiritual victory over you, down the road to the kingdom of the Most High God.

There and only there is peace, love, and life forever and ever. You can see the gates to His kingdom from afar; you can see its light, its divine light illumine your darkest night as you press forward on the road, passing stumbling block after stumbling block, down the road to your baptism on and on, down the road to be born again if it hasn't already occurred, closer and closer, brighter and brighter come the light.

"Blessed are those who do His commandments, that they may have the right to the tree of life and may enter through the gates into the city" (Rev. 21:14).

To some, myself included, the thought of being a Christian was a feeling. Maybe the thought generated this feeling, but for sure the feeling persisted with the thought that if I were to follow Christ and His commandments, His laws, and His statutes that I would be subject to the dictates of some alien or foreign power.

And this feeling then generated a fear of going into the unknown and fear so strong it stops the impulse to go deeper into the word of God. Then came that day that I was entirely alone. I knew deep within myself that it was over. My life was not my own. I was drowning in my own ignorance, people condemning me from all directions, falling into depressions, and yet even in this completely horrid mental and physical state, I could not even start to analyze my condition. Staying drunk and out of touch with reality, not eating, having no money, no home, no friends, no family—everything I tried to do turned to mud in my hands.

In those days I began to pray dumbly, with no self-justification. There was no hope left in me, no hope in the days ahead, no hope for today or tomorrow. What was certain yesterday was impossible to reach today. Do I take my own life? Do I just give up and call it quits? I had to make a decision. Stay or leave? So in the silence of an old barn that I was sleeping in, I made the decision. I had given Satan fifty years of my life, now I would give God fifty years, and now I could see who the liar is.

So in complete theological ignorance I repented. My attention was not on Christ, and I concentrated on Him as judge, father, savior, the truth, and now sought for His love and His love only. I prayed, I prayed with hope, I repented asking forgiveness for all the days of unbelief over the years of sin and pleasures of the outside world.

I read the Bible, not understanding a word, so I read it again and again and again. Why did God love certain people? Why did He love David? King David took another man's wife and killed her husband, yet God forgave him and loved him. Why did God pick certain men to do His work? Why did He pick Samuel, Isaiah? Why Daniel, Ezekiel, Hosea, Esther, Ruth, Jeremiah, and Elisha? Why did Christ pick Matthew, Mark, Luke, John, and Paul; of all people to pick from, he chose Paul, who was Saul.

This is one of the most vivid phenomena of our spiritual walk. So simple yet undetected. Saul, the worldly person, highly intellectual, born and raised with the best intentions, admired by the anti-Christ crowd, his expectations to hold the Christians responsible for all of the evils of that time period and sets about scrutinizing their recent conduct. Saul was not conscious of the fact he was in the presence of the Lord. Neither was I, neither are many of us today as we board our clattering train every day expecting a lasting bliss only to see it fade away by nightfall, and we withdraw into our conditioned space. For some of us, it seems to be dark, cold, dry, and dead. Why do I find myself exhausted from seeking and expecting the joy the world promises me every day only to find it suddenly vanish and I find nothing can comfort my heart?

Saul was on his way to embarrass the Christians in Damascus when Christ spiritually struck Him from his horse, blinded him physically, and appeared to him spiritually. From that moment on for the rest of his life, he endured suffering and hardships. However, because of his spiritual position and condition, he gained inward courage to rejoice when enduring those hardships and sufferings. He gained wisdom to understand God's will for his life and gained determination to follow the narrow path of truth and love of Christ. He gained this wisdom of God through his fear and his repentance. He was able to see his past sins, repenting and asking for reformation.

And it was with this before me on that day I struggled to commit myself to spirituality. I trembled with fear. I was unworthy of forgiveness. I knew I could never ever reach the plateau, the spiritual plateau, of these men. But, could I start at the bottom, asking God to please let me start at the bottom? Lord Jesus Christ, Son of God, have mercy on me, a sinner. I wanted to start at the bottom. Please just let me start to find a life with You, Christ; with You, Father, the Creator and the Holy Spirit, the very spirit of God Himself.

This is the self-emptying, my confession, our confessing, our self-condemnation, every black spot on my life, I repent, please forgive me. If we say we are not sinful, then we deceive ourselves. How many times did I reassure myself with the voice from within, "Nobody saw me, nobody saw us, right? No one knows what we think or do.

> But there is nothing covered up that will not be revealed, and hidden that will not be known. Accordingly, whatever you have said in the dark shall be heard in the light and what you have whispered in the inner rooms shall be proclaimed upon the housetops. (Luke 12:2–3)

Consequently, the old saying about "someone is always watching" is true. As your life starts to change, your old self departing and your real self, new to you, is emerging you will become more and more aware of the fact that you are being watched.

You will see those that are faithful and those that are foolish. Those that choose the light and those that continue to choose the darkness. Repentance results will be total pardon or remission of your sins; it is total forgiveness, and it will free you from your sin nature, your passions. Why? Because repentance is the only way healing will come. Your new strength will come to you and I who are caught up in sin.

"Repent therefore and return, that your sins may be wiped away, in order that times of refreshing may come from the presence of the Lord" (Acts 3:19). As we have stated many times before, when the Lord enters into our life, our internal life, His presence is a cleansing, incredible confrontation with sin, bringing a refreshing spiritual awakening within our soul and spirit. His presence in our inner house opens doors, turns on lights, opens windows, and a fresh wind sets the gift of our inheritance at our feet.

"For I will be merciful to their iniquities and I will remember their sins no more" (Heb. 8:12). Now do not forget what the Lord speaks is an absolute, and therefore, when you have given Him your heavy burden and He promises you rest and peace, then believe it, let it go—all of it; keep none of it. Our biggest problem many times is we hang around our train wreck crying and weeping about what we coulda, woulda, shoulda done. Let the Holy Spirit burn the wreck. He will give you comfort and peace. Trust in Him and He, the Holy One, will empower you and guide you through your battlegrounds and minefields.

One of my biggest obstacles was to get free from my past. I had this wagon I pulled around with me, behind me sometimes, beside me sometimes, and in front of me sometimes. Now this wagon was filled with the things of my past, and at times I would let myself float back there and have a pity party. Woe is me, and I would dig deeper and feel worse.

One day I had a vision of sitting in a wagon full of rotten manures, throwing it in the air, and the deeper I dug, the worse it smelled and the sicker I became, and the air around me was full of darkness because of my head being stuck in the center of this wagon full of my past sins and guilt set there helping me become sicker.

Cut it loose! Don't go back there and set in your old sin nature and wish for the very things that got you into trouble in the first place. People say, "Well, you don't understand," "I just can't over it," "It just bugs me all the time," "I know I'm not forgiven, I just know it!"

Visualize pulling your wagon of the past up on a high mountaintop, the rope that has you tied to the wagon, pull out your sharp spiritual knife and cut the rope. The wagon full of your past sins picks up speed in its downward plunge and disappears into the darkness below. Start your walk toward Christ free form that awful constant battle over guilt and rejection.

You are free, your repentance sets you free, it's an absolute, a spiritual absolute, and when your mind starts to be harassed by some hellish thoughts, then speak up, rebuke it in the name of Jesus Christ. You are not the only one who struggles with these things. It is your spiritual warfare, your determination to become free; spiritual and knowledgeable, loving, kind, and gentle; rid yourself of hypocrisy, seeking truth and love of God.

Lord Jesus Christ, Son of God, have mercy on me, a sinner.